HUMAN ENERGY

PIERRE TEILHARD DE CHARDIN

HUMAN
ENERGY

Translated by J. M. Cohen

A HELEN AND KURT WOLFF BOOK
HARCOURT BRACE JOVANOVICH, INC.
New York

Originally published in 1962 by Editions du Seuil under the title *L'Energie humaine*

ISBN 0-15-142390-3
Library of Congress Catalog Card Number: 79-139231
Printed in the United States of America

CONTENTS

FOREWORD

In the previously published volumes of the works of Teilhard de Chardin, the different essays he left, in so far as they did not form an entire volume, were grouped around some great theme such as the theory of evolution in general (*The Vision of the Past*), the emergence of man (*The Appearance of Man*), and hopes for the future resulting from a study of the past (*The Future of Man*).

Among his unpublished writings bearing on his 'phenomenology', however, are a number of essays that could not be collected in the previous volumes, but are nevertheless of the first importance for the sound understanding of his teaching. They are perhaps some of the most original and valuable expositions that he made. These small works are now gathered, in chronological order, into two volumes entitled *Human Energy* and *The Activation of Human Energy*.

Undoubtedly, many ideas will be found in these writings that have already been elaborated from another angle in essays already published. But these ideas are here developed in greater detail; they are notably filled out and explored in greater depth. They therefore make an invaluable contribution to the understanding of Teilhard's vision, the inner coherence and almost inexhaustible fecundity of which are here displayed anew.

It will become increasingly evident that Teilhard's work as a whole has a profound unity and develops a primary intuition. On the occasion of a lecture on the subject of 'The Philosophical Intuition' given at Bologna on 10 April, 1911, Henri Bergson strikingly demonstrated that there are two ways of approaching a philosopher's work: 'A philosophical system seems at first to stand up like a complete building of skilful architecture, in which arrangements have been made for the comfortable accommodation of all problems. It is possible to consider this edifice from the outside, to go all round it, to examine each of its features separately and identify the materials used by its maker and the source from which he obtained them. This method may be useful, though it tells us very little about its internal coherence and the motives that determined its overall conception.

'There is however a second way of approach to a thinker's work. This is to penetrate to the very heart of the building, "to take our place in the philosopher's mind." Then the system undergoes a total transformation. The coherence and necessity of all its elements become suddenly perceptible. "Then everything converges to a single point, to which we feel we can draw closer and closer, though we must despair of ever reaching it".[1] All this very largely applies to the work of Teilhard de Chardin. In his case also, it is not enough to consider his work from outside and examine the elements of which it is built one by one, though this analysis may be useful. It is much more important to make the effort to study his work in some way from within, and discover the central point from which the author has built and which has given him perpetual new inspirations.

Putting aside his theological writings, it is apparent that the point of departure of Teilhard's whole work is the wish to penetrate as deeply as possible into the fundamental structure of the universe in which we live and of which we form part. More than any other philosopher, he took the findings of the sciences as his starting point, since these enabled him to grasp the world in its historical dimension. From this point of view—which to him became evidential—he tried to discover the inner coherence and essential direction of universal history, which, despite the multitude and diversity of phenomena, reveals to his eyes a fundamen-

[1] H. Bergson, 'La pensée et le mouvant' (1934), Oeuvres (centenary edition), 1939, pp. 1346-7.

tal unity and harmony which guide even our activity as men in that direction.

All his essays start from this primal conviction and try to show us the nature of that fundamental unity and the prospects it opens up on human existence. Bergson's words apply also to him: 'The whole complexity of his teaching, which might stretch to infinity, is therefore only the incommensurability between his simple intuition and the means of expressing it that are at his disposal.'[1] I do not think we should be far from Teilhard's primal intuition if we were to seek it in the neighbourhood of what he called the law of progressive complexity and increasing consciousness, in other words the problem of the relation between spirit and matter.

Impelled by his desire to see the world as a unity, Teilhard was compelled to ask the following question. 'How can the two realms of our experience, those of the outer and inner world, be brought to a unity within the framework of an evolutionary universe?' At first sight this might seem a purely philosophical problem. For centuries past, it is the philosophers who have drawn parallels permitting an approach to it. However the way in which Teilhard de Chardin sets about solving the problem is not primarily philosophical, although his ideas undoubtedly open up metaphysical prospects in the end.

Teilhard chose his point of departure in the findings of science, and he appeals to hypotheses of a scientific type. In this realm he adopts the theory of the dual character of the *Weltstoff*, or stuff of the universe. If we adopt the hypothesis that everything has a without and (virtually at least) a within, and that these two aspects of reality evolve throughout history towards an ever growing complexity/consciousness, the universe begins to become a coherent and intelligible reality to us, which it will never do without this hypothesis.

In the author's opinion this is no question of founding a philosophical theory, but exclusively of a scientific working hypo-

[1]*ibid.*

thesis. This position is of capital importance. Teilhard de Chardin certainly does not begin from any sort of philosophical pan-psychism. Being used to a scientific method of thought, he constructs a provisional hypothesis, which he subsequently compares with reality. So, in the scientific manner, the hypothesis, according to Teilhard, derives its whole value and power from the harmony and coherence it supplies as soon as it is accepted.

He therefore ceaselessly strives to examine the results produced by this hypothesis when confronted with reality, and the further he explored in this direction the more convinced he became that he had found the key to a sound understanding of the universe, and in particular of the place occupied by man in that universe. It is not surprising therefore to see him continually returning to this theme and applying it in all directions.

In so far as Teilhard is working on the scientific plane, it is not difficult to accept his arguments. No one can object to an attempt of this sort. Difficulties only occur when one faces the task of interpreting the results obtained by this kind of work from a philosophical point of view. It cannot of course be denied that sooner or later this task is unavoidable, since the question is bound to arise: To what extent can these arguments be reconciled with traditional philosophy?

Teilhard de Chardin was conscious of the philosophical repercussions of his ideas. In a letter to a friend and colleague, to whom he sent his *Sketch of a Personalistic Universe*, he wrote: 'I am going to send you my latest essay in which I have attempted a brief synthesis of the question. This essay runs the risk of conflicting with your metaphysics at several points. But I am certain that a more traditional interpretation of my view is possible. The role of my paradoxes may be to call urgent attention to the points on which classical philosophy needs either to be widened or made more flexible.' (Letter of 15 August, 1938).

It is clear from this passage that in Teilhard's opinion, classical philosophy (there can be no doubt that it was the Aristotelian metaphysics of the Scholastics that he had in mind) needs supplementing and extending at certain points, but that it is substantially compatible with his ideas. On this last point we have the vital evidence of a highly qualified philosopher, Père Maréchal, s.j. In a letter to Père Auguste Valensin, s.j., he wrote in these terms: 'As in his works, the author presumes that a certain continuity of evolution from matter to man is admissible. This can be understood in a perfectly orthodox sense and indeed fits easily into the Aristotelian theories of causality . . . Believing that the spiritual soul is only created *"in corpore"*, and only operates in conjunction with matter, they (the philosophers and theologians) automatically accept a "noosphere" linked with the rest of the material world by necessary correlations. There is therefore in their view a "natural science" not only of the human body but of the entire man. This natural determinism of the whole man does not exclude spontaneity, even in its highest expression; a free act.'

The essays published in this volume will undoubtedly give rise to discussion in this field, and thus stimulate and enrich further research. The essays touching on this particular question therefore must be considered principally as a working tool which may be useful for a subsequent examination of the problem raised. According to the author's own intentions, they must be equally considered as a provisional contribution to the solution of a problem which has already occupied men's minds for a very long time, and will perhaps never be completely solved.

This statement presents the general problem of the relationship of Teilhard's thought to scholastic philosophy. Although developed from a phenomenological standpoint, his arguments lead in the long run to a metaphysic. The opposite would be quite unimaginable. His analysis of the cosmic phenomenon leads us to the threshold of philosophical thought, throws a new light on old problems and even indicates the direction in which this philosophical thought should be carried further. Jean Daniélou, s.j., recently underlined this point in a striking manner: 'One has the feeling that he rediscovers metaphysics as the Pre-Socrates must have discovered them at the beginning. He builds a metaphysic as an extension of the science of his day.'[1] Exactly so. By going back to the living sources of a true metaphysic, that is to say to a complete recognition of reality, as it appears by the light of empirical science, Teilhard has opened the way to a renewal of philosophical reflection.

Here Père Daniélou points to one of Teilhard de Chardin's particular merits. Certainly, he was not always happy in the framework of traditional scholasticism. 'On the one hand, indisputably he felt hampered by it. His thought is never expressed in terms of the scholastic categories of action and potentiality, matter and form, substance and accident. Teilhard definitely wants to start afresh from zero, that is to say base himself on his contact with the science of his day. He belongs to the age of nuclear physics, which has revolutionized our conception of matter by showing that matter and energy are interchangeable, and that matter can therefore be considered as a field of energetic forces. He belongs to the age in which biological evolution has shown itself the most acceptable explanation of a collection of facts, and a law that makes them intelligible. Teilhard's language is the language of this science, which differs from the language of traditional scholasticism.'

What is the philosophical significance of Teilhard de Chardin? That he universalizes the language of the sciences and extends it to the whole of existence: 'He translates the scientific categories into metaphysical categories ... His thought can be interpreted in this sense: that at different levels of existence we find analogies which reveal a certain resemblance. Teilhard thus isolates some general laws of life; the law of *complexification*, the law of *evolution*, the law of *personalization*, the law of *socialization*. These laws can be verified at all levels. They therefore enable us to think in terms of a totality, to establish links. Metaphysics is precisely this. No metaphysics without analogies. Now modern

[1] J. Daniélou, 'Signification de Teilhard de Chardin,' *Études*, Feb. 1962, vol. 312, p. 147.

thought too often fails to recognize the value of analogies for the gaining of knowledge.'

Considered in this way, Teilhard de Chardin's work has indeed an outstanding philosophical significance. But at the same time it is evident how closely and to what an important extent the sequence of his ideas is linked to Aristotelian and Thomist philosophy: 'This also begins with a physical and biological analysis, and its metaphysical truths are conceived analogically by an extension of this analysis. Teilhard thus appears to go back to the basic attitudes of the traditional philosophy of the Church, but divests it, one might say, of a language belonging to an out-of-date science, and invents for it a new language expressive of modern science. But if this was possible, for Teilhard, it was because he had inherited the scholastic philosophy and preserved its essentials. It was this that saved him from materialism, pantheism and evolutionism. The categories of personality, creation and God which constitute his thought belong to scholasticism. But he has only retained its basic categories. He has interpreted it in terms of the scientific findings of his day.'[1]

We have quoted this passage in its entirety because it eminently expresses the philosophical bearing of Teilhard de Chardin's work, and at the same time saves us from making too hasty a judgement of the acceptability or non-acceptability of his ideas. For Père Daniélou clearly shows that on a higher plane Teilhard remained faithful to the spirit of the scholastic and Aristotelian mode of thought. Indeed his faithfulness was infinitely more real than if it had taken the form of a simple repetition of traditional phrases. It is not his least achievement that he thus re-established the links between metaphysics and the sciences, for their connexion is too easily lost sight of.

We should be exceeding our task were we to attempt to comment here on the various problems raised by Teilhard de Chardin in the essays contained in these books. They would require a full and deep discussion and perhaps on certain points they might

[1]ibid., pp. 147-8.

demand criticism. But before attempting this task, we must first study his writings with all necessary attention and view his conclusions in their true light, which, alas, has not always been done in the past. We venture to hope that the essays here collected will be received in the spirit that inspired them, and that they will afford precious help to all those who are trying to find a real solution, in so far as this is within our power, of the great questions raised by the existence of man.

N. M. WILDIERS

INTRODUCTORY NOTE

The essays published in this and succeeding volumes were not revised for publication by Teilhard de Chardin. We present them in accordance with his intention and, as explained by Dr. Wildiers in his foreword, as 'working tools'. The notes in this volume have been rendered necessary by erroneous interpretations of the author's thought in various books and articles in the press. Whenever possible we have taken our explanations from Teilhard's own writings.

THE SPIRIT OF THE EARTH

INTRODUCTION

The following pages are not immediately intended for the defence of any orthodoxy, either scientific or religious. They are simply trying to express in all sincerity a particular view of the world.

At the present time many believers, to avoid the anxieties that contact with reality might renew in them, allow a veil of conventional answers to cover the mysteries of life. And scientists, engrossed in the investigation of detail or caught up by a false materialism, apparently fail to see that by virtue of their discoveries the fundamental question of the future confronts us in all our activities. Stifled by the words they have invented, men are in danger of losing sight of the problem. They have reached the point of no longer grasping the meaning of what their own experiments are discovering.

Basing myself on what I have learnt in fifty years from science and religion, I have tried to rise above this situation. I have endeavoured to come out of the fog and obtain a view of things in themselves. And this is what I believe I have seen—confronting the world alone.[1]

[1] Teilhard had been considering this essay ever since 1926, when he wrote to Canon Gaudefroy: 'I am thinking of a kind of "Account of the Earth", in which I shall speak not as a Frenchman, not as a unit in any group, but as a man, simply as a "terrestrian". I want to express the confidence, desires and plenitude, also the disappointments, worries and a kind of vertigo of a man who considers the destinies and interests of the earth (humanity) as a whole.'

I SPIRIT OR MATTER

The first thing I saw was that man alone can help man to decipher the world. Up to now, man in his essential characteristics has been omitted from all scientific theories of nature. For some, his 'spiritual' value is too high to allow of his being included, without some sort of sacrilege, in a general scheme of history. For others his power of choosing and abstracting is too far removed from material determinisms for it to be possible, or even useful, to associate him with the elements composing the physical sciences. In both cases, either through excessive admiration or lack of esteem, man is left floating above, or left on the edge of the universe. He is either uprooted or supernumerary. The scientist himself stands apart from the objects of science. This is the cause of all our present intellectual and moral difficulties. We shall never understand either man or nature unless, as the facts demand, we completely replace man (without destroying him) in nature.

This we must at last do. We must accept what science tells us, that man was born from the earth. But, more logical than the scientists who lecture us, we must carry this lesson to its conclusion: that is to say accept that man was born entirely from the world—not only his flesh and bones but his incredible power of thought.[1]

Let us consider him, without reducing his stature, as a phenomenon. This will *ipso facto* change the face of the universe.

The point of departure for this metamorphosis is that life, manifested in man, reveals itself as a property *sui generis* of the cosmos. In the history of the physical sciences, there are periodic

[1]For the Christian transformist, God's creative action is no longer conceived as an intrusive thrusting of His works into the midst of pre-existent beings, but as a *bringing to birth* of the successive stages of His work in the heart of things. It is no less essential, no less universal, no less intimate either on that account. (Author's note on 'The Transformist Paradox', *The Vision of the Past*, p. 102.)

discoveries of 'characteristic phenomena' which by their apparent anomaly reveal a fundamental property of things. Among these have been the activity of radium and the inability of experiment to detect a movement of the globe through the ether.[1] The greatest mistake that science could have made when confronted with these facts would have been to consign them to the realm of tiresome freaks. If we had done so we should have no knowledge of the vast realm of radiations, and the far-reaching theories of relativity. Man 'the thinker', generally regarded as an 'irregularity' in the universe, is precisely one of those special phenomena by which one of the most basic aspects of the cosmos is revealed to us with a degree of intensity that renders it immediately recognizable. Below man, life, despite the singular properties of its constituents and its general evolution, might at a pinch have been consigned to an obscure department of chemistry. By confining it, most artificially moreover, to its lowest and most mechanical terms (that is to say to forms scarcely emerged from, or in process of re-immersion in matter) biology might attempt to reduce it to tactisms and tropisms. With man something new, which science had hitherto been able to contain if only by violent means, burst forth irresistibly. At the level of humanity, there can be no more temporizing. We must make up our minds, by virtue of the general perspectives of evolution themselves, to make a special place in the physics of the universe for the powers of consciousness, spontaneity and improbability represented by life. This is inevitable, or man remains unexplained—excluded from a cosmos of which he manifestly forms a part. But then, and this is the *second step* towards the light, the moment one tries to determine this place it inevitably proves both vast and fundamental. Life, in fact, is not a partial, limited property of matter, analogous to some vibratory or molecular effect: it is rather a sort of inverse of everything that habitually serves us as a definition of matter. Consequently life is not a fixed and static relationship between elements of the world; it clearly appears, on the con-

[1]An absolute movement through inter-sidereal space.

trary, as the sign of a universal process; terrestrial life being a function of the sidereal evolution of the globe, which is itself a function of total cosmic evolution. Hence the dilemma: either life, completed by thought, is merely an illusion in the world, or else, once it is granted the least physical reality, it tends to occupy a universal, central and exigent position in it. *This is the true scientific situation.*

Once life has encroached so far, only one reality (in so far as it truly exists) remains to confront it, and can be compared to it in size and universality: this is entropy, that mysterious *involution* by which the world tends progressively to refurl on itself, in unorganized plurality and increasing probability, the layer of cosmic energy. And then, before our enquiring minds, a final duel is fought between life (thought) and entropy (matter) for the domination of the universe. Are life and entropy the two opposite but equivalent faces of a single fundamental reality in eternal equipoise? Or radically has one of them the natural advantage of being more primal and durable than the other?

Later we shall show by a critical study of the conditions of human activity, that unless the universe contains internal contradictions, it seems to demand that life shall be guaranteed a boundless future; that is to say will escape the complete mastery of the forces of retreat. Life would not be liveable if it were not conscious of being, at least partially, irreversible, and therefore superior to the inverse attractions of entropy.

Here another argument, drawn from the laws not of action but of human thought (the offspring of the world), will be enough roughly to decide our choice. Instinctively, in their attempts to make an intellectual scheme of the universe, many men try to use matter as their *starting point.* Because matter can be touched, and because it *appears* historically to have existed first, it is accepted without examination as the primordial stuff and most intelligible portion of the cosmos. But *this road leads nowhere.* Not only does matter, the symbol for multiplicity and transience, escape the direct grasp of thought, but, more disadvantageously still, this same matter shows itself incapable by its very nature of giving rise to the world that surrounds us and gives us substance. It is radically impossible to conceive that 'interiorized' and spontaneous elements could ever have developed from a universe presumed in its initial state to have consisted entirely of determinisms. Anyone who accepts this starting point blocks all roads that would bring him back to the present state of the universe. On the other hand, from a cosmos initially formed and made up of elementary 'freedoms', it is easy to deduce, by virtue of the effect of large numbers and habitual behaviour, all the appearances of exactitude upon which the mathematical physics of matter is founded. A universe whose primal stuff is matter is irremediably fixed and sterile; whereas a universe of 'spiritual' stuff has all the elasticity it would need to lend itself both to evolution (life) and to involution (entropy). This consideration must be enough to decide our intellectual choice.

No, the cosmos could not possibly be explained as a dust of unconscious elements, on which life, for some incomprehensible reason, burst into flower—as an accident or as a mould. But it is *fundamentally and primarily* living, and its complete history is ultimately nothing but an immense psychic exercise; the slow but progressive attaining of a diffused consciousness—a gradual escape from the 'material' conditions which, *secondarily*, veil it in an initial state of extreme plurality. From this point of view man is nothing but the point of emergence in nature, at which this deep cosmic evolution culminates and declares itself. From this point onwards man ceases to be a spark fallen by chance on earth and coming from another place. He is the flame of a general fermentation of the universe[1] which breaks out suddenly on the earth. He is no longer a sterile enigma or discordant note in

[1]Sustained, of course, by some deep creative force. If we do not speak more explicitly of this force, it is, we repeat, because our purpose is to follow the shape of the apparent curve of phenomena without examining the metaphysical conditions of its existence. (Author's note on the subject of 'Hominization', *The Vision of the Past*, p. 73.)

nature. He is the key of things and the final harmony. In him everything takes shape and is explained.

The world is like a maze before us. Many entrances, but only one path that leads to the centre. Because we approach at the wrong angle or from the wrong direction nature resists our efforts to reach it. Let us make a better choice of our known and unknown quantities. Let us put our x in the proper place, that is to say in the material and the plural; and let us recognize that *evidences of consciousness and freedom are primordial and defy analysis*. Then we find the right order. No more closed doors or blind alleys. The Ariadne's thread that can guide us through the universe is the 'birth of the spirit', and the hand from which we receive it is the faithful recognition of the 'phenomenon of man'.

II THE EARTH AND THE SPIRIT

So, our thought has made its choice: the genesis of the spirit is a cosmic phenomenon; and the cosmos consists in this same genesis.[1] Life is dormant everywhere in the cosmos, but the only life we

[1]'As in his other works, the author assumes as acceptable a certain continuity of evolution from matter to man. This can be understood in a perfectly orthodox way, and falls quite easily within the framework of the Aristotelian theories of causality . . .

'Believing that the spiritual soul is *only* created *in corpore*, and only operates in conjunction with matter, they (the Thomist philosophers) automatically admit a "noosphere", linked with the rest of the material world by necessary correlations. There is therefore, in their view, a "natural science" not only of the human body, but of the entire man. This natural determinism of the whole man does not exclude spontaneity, even in its highest expression, a free act or action.'

(Extract from a revision made by Père Maréchal, s.j., of an essay by Teilhard de Chardin entitled 'Le Phénomène Humain' (The Phenomenon of Man) and dated 1928. Teilhard sent this revision to Père Valensin in a letter of 29 September, 1928. This note is repeated in the foreword. [*Ed.*])

24

know so far is life on earth. Let us try to understand the *life of the earth.*

It has been said (and certain astronomers are seemingly reverting to the idea) that the earth might well be the only centre in the universe that is at present alive. We will not discuss this most improbable and undemonstrable privilege attributed to our planet. But we must point in passing to a particularly pernicious way of interpreting this idea, by making life, under these circumstances, a marvellous *accident*, produced once and for all outside cosmic evolution by an extraordinary chance. The point of view to which we have for sound scientific and philosophical reasons attached ourselves deals justly with this childish interpretation and corrects it. No, even if life was, and had to remain, peculiar to the earth, it would not follow that it was 'accidental' to the world. We should simply have to conclude that, in the sidereal expanses, the terrestrial centre alone (or at least first) became ready to localize a possibility *in a state of universal suspension,* and that this possibility has *evolved there complete.* Life and thought might then be peculiar to the earth; but they would still be the life and thought of the world.

Geologists are still uncertain of the way in which the individualization of the earth took place. It was in any case an agglomeration of elementary particles. Let us look at this star at its birth. The first idea to get into our minds at this moment is the extraordinary richness and complexity of its 'juvenile matter': a magma in which, besides many physico-chemical activities today neutralized or evaporated, there floated in a form at present inaccessible to our investigators the *influences of pre-life.* It has been rightly observed that the most 'primitive' peoples at present living on earth are only static and exhausted groups in which we can no longer find any of the fire that animated the advance guard of humanity when it was passing through this same cultural stage. Similarly no terrestrial matter accessible to our present day investigations can give us an exact idea of the *original earth.* Something departed from it (suddenly and once and for all, no doubt) when the veil of the biosphere, infinitely complex from its origins, spread over the surface of the globe. It is often asked why 'spontaneous generation' today seems impossible. The present sterility of matter is attributed to a variety of causes: modifications of climate, of solar radiation or of the atmosphere. In our view, the most important thing is that at the first appearance of life we encounter a phenomenon that is linked with the total evolution of the earth: there is one season, and one alone for this event in the history of any one planet. The 'juvenile earth' contained a *quantum of consciousness*;[1] and this quantum passed completely into the biosphere. Thereafter, terrestrial matter is capable of sustaining and nourishing life, but cannot give rise to new life. It is exhausted, bled dry, 'devitalized'. To make life, scientists would have to make a new earth.

Now let us follow the inner movements of the layer of life by which our earth was palpably enveloped. What is happening in the layers of the biosphere which will henceforth be the only ones to interest us? Here the history of life becomes free of simple hypotheses and begins to answer us—provided we can understand. In our time, the fundamental link between living forms, and their birth one from another are no longer seriously disputed. But biologists are still far from agreeing about the shape of this evolution, in which many still see only an unintelligible proliferation and disorderly diversification. This uncertainty undoubtedly stems from the confusion still commonly reigning

---

[1]'The possible existence must be admitted of a psychism so diluted as to have no more than a very distant relationship with what this word denotes on the human or even the animal scale.'

This psychism is 'a state of consciousness' which will enable one or another material structure, at certain moments and in certain regions of space and time, to behave in such a way as to betray (albeit very vaguely) a sort of prevision of the immediate future, that is to say the knowledge of what act to perform in order to reach forward towards a previously determined goal. (Jean E. Charon, *La Connaissance de l'Univers*, Paris, Editions du Seuil, 1962, pp. 136 and 139.)

regarding three very different types of biological evolution. The most superficial of these evolutions (which might be called *evolution by dispersion*) effectively consists of a simple diversification (or spreading) of living forms within a spindle of equal possibilities of form or colouring, among these forms are certain groups of plants, moths and butterflies, fish and antelopes. Below this lies *evolution of instrumental differentiation*, by which forms are distributed along various radiations, each defined by the acquisition of a specialized morphological type (swimming, running, flight—burrowers and creatures of prey). From these transformations are born the majority of the 'phyla' identified by palaeontology. Finally, far below this, there appears the *evolution of greater consciousness*, by virtue of which living beings, in the mass, along *the whole front* of the biosphere, raise themselves more or less (with the exception of fixed or regressive types) towards greater organization (individual or collective) and towards greater spontaneity. Well, only this third kind of evolution (expressed both in the concentration of nervous systems and the formation of social groups) can give us the *direction and true shape of the movements of life*. Up to now biology, in forming theories, has scarcely noticed, scarcely studied the 'evolution of consciousness', hardly fitted by its very scope to provide points of support for systematics. Yet in this undoubtedly lies the *basic movement* of which the other two types of evolution are no more than harmonics. In it alone we at last possess an *absolute measure* for the developments not only of life on earth but of the world. Like a mounting tide, the multiple flow towards consciousness swells with its sap and drives forward, with no complete recoil or deviation, all the fibres of the biosphere. Its successive impulses mark the great stages of life. And one day along the axis of its progress the breakthrough was made into a new realm. After thousands of centuries of effort, life on earth, the child of the cosmos, emerged into *thought*.

And here we return to the principal event dominating the natural history of the world: the phenomenon of man. And a number of essential characteristics must strike our attention when we confront it.

First of all man (that is to say thinking life) established himself on earth *by way of a critical point or area of transformation*. Like the apex without magnitude in which the sections of a cone become finally concentrated; like the vapour into which a liquid turns at boiling point without change of temperature, thought succeeds unreflective life by crossing a threshold, by a change of state. Certainly nothing of the kind had happened in our world since the initial condensation of pre-life. Human thought therefore introduces a new era in the history of nature. But *though it is a renewal of life it is not an entirely new life*. In its spirituality, as at the apex of a cone, all the productive forces of the past, *recognizable though hominized*—hunger, love, the sense of struggle, the lust for prey—must appear again. To control these inherited characteristics at a higher level is the task of morality and the secret of 'higher life'.

From another point of view, the biodynamical consequences of the appearance of thought in the biosphere reproduce, in a higher realm, those of the first appearance of organic life. At the birth of the biosphere the 'juvenile' qualities of terrestrial matter, which thereafter became incapable of producing more life, were breathed into the universe. In the opening on its stem of the human flower, animal life in its turn probably exhausted all its power of 'reflexion'. Consequently no other thought could ever arise on earth beside human thought, either as a competitor or an ally. And no other thought could come to replace it either, if by some general desertion or disappearance it should ever be cut off. Hence this conclusion—scientifically based, we think, and inevitable: In the human spirit, as in a single irreplaceable fruit, the whole life of earth—that is to say, in brief, its whole cosmic value—is gathered and sublimated.

III THE SPIRIT OF THE EARTH

One of the most important aspects of hominization, from the point of view of the history of life, is the accession of biological realities (or values) to the domain of moral realities (or values). From man onwards and in man, evolution has taken reflective consciousness of itself. Henceforth it can to some degree recognize its position in the world, choose its direction, and withhold its efforts. These new conditions open on earth the immense question of duty and its modalities. Why act—and how to act? All the rest of this study will, in effect, be nothing but a sketch of the *cosmic problem of action*.

So long as our conceptions of the universe remained static, the basis of duty remained extremely obscure. To account for this mysterious law which weighs fundamentally on our liberty, men had recourse to all sorts of explanations, from that of an explicit command issued from outside to that of an irrational but categorical instinct. In a spiritually evolutionary scheme of the universe, such as we have here accepted, the answer is quite simple. For the human unit the *initial* basis of obligation is the fact of being born and developing *as a function of a cosmic stream.* We must act, and in a certain way, because our individual destinies are dependent on a universal destiny. Duty, in its origin, is nothing but the reflexion of the universe in the atom.

But now, more precisely, in what concrete direction—along what exact plane—must we actively and freely extend, beyond our present state, the generative forces of the world?

Here, by virtue of its new attributes, new-born humanity is faced with a series of essential questions, which cannot be satisfactorily answered by a simple backward glance. In the development of life up to man, the individual seems always to have been definitely subordinated to the species. Its principal value was that of an agent of transmission, a point on the road. Life's task, it seems, was to achieve, by means of increasingly organized elements, the establishment on earth of a higher form of consciousness, a *state of personality*. With man and in man, the perfected and centred element, that is to say the *person*, is finally constituted. Will not values find their centre of gravity shifted by this basic event? Up to that point the unit existed for the mass. Henceforth will not the mass exist for the unit? To be brief, we are confronted with two theoretical possibilities: either from man onwards life comes to an absolute peak and scatters in a plurality of reflective consciousness, each of which is its own final reason; or beyond man (beyond the area of hominization), and despite the decisive and definitive value of 'personality', the unity of the evolutionary front remains intact, and the value of the world continues to be built up *ahead by a communal effort*. Two conceptions of evolution, and therefore two moralities.

In default of really precise philosophical or scientific reasons, a number of elementary instincts and fine feelings argue in favour of a pluralist structure of the human layer. Justifiably, to centre, individualize and personalize oneself is half the joy of life (the other and better half being, as we shall repeat, to decentre oneself in a being greater than oneself). We understand now that individuals, like nations, are naturally inclined to stop and pitch their tents on the first summit conquered. To disguise this idle egotism, there is no lack of systems that speciously exalt the unique value of the present moment (understood as an absolute closed on itself). We consider that this way of looking at the world—a particular favourite in literary and artistic circles—is simply infantile and rudimentary, and does not stand up to a serious analysis of the structure of things. Let the human individual, newly arrived on the great waters of life, enjoy in his first moment of exaltation the intoxication of raising himself to the highest point of the universe. The temptation is quite natural. But let him beware! Despite, or rather because of the autonomy he has attained, he is always dominated by another, higher unity from which he cannot free himself on pain of death. Precious though it is, the human monad remains vitally subjected to the law that, before his coming, obliged units to preserve and promote the whole in preference to themselves. First of all, even supposing that he could find fulfilment in himself, the human individual would still have to let humanity pass ahead of him since from humanity there will constantly be born monads at least equal to himself. But, if he is honest, he will have to recognize that in reality his own 'person' is insufficient for him, and that the most valuable part of his being is precisely what he is still expecting from the unrealized part of the universe. Humanity, for each of us, is not only that stem which supports, unifies, preserves. It is the leading shoot which contains the achievements of the future. Man must believe in humanity more than in himself, or else he will lose hope.

Thus, on the level of man (or, as one might say, of the noosphere) the progressive advance of earthly life does not fragmentate. Unities of a new kind are formed, to act as more perfect constituents and intended for a superior organization. The general convergence which constitutes universal evolution is not completed by hominization. There are not only minds on the earth. *The world continues and there will be a spirit of the earth.*

But now, if this picture is not a dream—that is to say, if we twentieth-century humans are indeed, scientifically speaking, nothing but the elements of a soul seeking itself through the cosmos—what is the purpose of our absurd objections, our childish interests? Why do we argue and doze and bore ourselves? Why do we hesitate to open our hearts wide to the call of the world within us, to the *sense of the earth*?

IV THE SENSE OF THE EARTH

By 'sense of the earth' we mean here the passionate sense of common destiny that draws the thinking fraction of life ever further forward. Rightly, no feeling is better founded in nature, and therefore more powerful, than this one. But in fact, none is slower to awake either, since in order to become explicit, it requires that our consciousness, rising above the growing (but still much too limited) circles of family, country and race, shall finally discover that the *only truly natural and real human unity* is the spirit of the earth. For hundreds of centuries (up to yesterday, one might say) men have lived as children, without understanding the mystery of their birth or the secret of the obscure urges which sometimes reach them in great waves from the deep places of the world. Impelled by the succession of discoveries which in the space of the last century have revealed to our generation first the extent and significance of duration, then the limitless spiritual resources of matter, and finally the power of living beings in association, our psychology seems to be in course of changing, and man to be approaching what one might call his crisis of puberty. A new victorious passion is beginning (we seriously believe) to take shape which will sweep away or transform what have so far been the whims and childishness of the earth. And its salutary action has come just in time to 'control', arouse or order the newly freed energies of love, the dormant energies of human unity, the hesitant energies of research.

a Love. Love is the most universal, the most tremendous and the most mysterious of the cosmic forces. After centuries of tentative effort, social institutions have externally dyked and canalized it. Taking advantage of this situation, the moralists have tried to submit it to rules. But in constructing their theories they have never got beyond the level of an elementary empiricism influenced by out-of-date conceptions of matter and the relics of old taboos. Socially, in science, business and public affairs, men pretend not to know it, though under the surface it is everywhere. Huge, ubiquitous and always unsubdued—this wild force seems to have defeated all hopes of understanding and governing it. It is therefore allowed to run everywhere beneath our civilization. We are conscious of it, but all we ask of it is to amuse us, or not to harm us. Is it truly possible for humanity to continue to live and grow without asking itself how much truth and energy it is losing by neglecting its incredible power of love?

From the standpoint of spiritual evolution, which we here assume, it seems that we can give a name and value to this strange energy of love. Can we not say quite simply that in its essence it is the attraction exercised on each unit of consciousness by the centre of the universe in course of taking shape? It calls us to the great union, the realization of which is the only process at present taking place in nature. By this hypothesis, according to which (in agreement with the findings of psychological analysis) love is the primal and universal psychic energy, does not everything become clear around us, both for our minds and our actions? We may try to reconstruct the history of the world from outside by observing the play of atomic, molecular or cellular combinations in their various processes. We may attempt, still more efficaciously, this same task from within by following the progress made by conscious spontaneity and noting the successive stages achieved. The most telling and profound way of describing the evolution of the universe would undoubtedly be to trace the evolution of love.

In its most primitive forms, when life was scarcely individualized, love is hard to distinguish from molecular forces; one might think of it as a matter of chemisms or tactisms. Then little by little it becomes distinct, though still *confused* for a very long time with the simple function of reproduction. Not till hominization does it at last reveal the secret and manifold virtues of its violence. 'Hominized' love is distinct from all other love, because the 'spectrum' of its warm and penetrating light is marvellously enriched. No longer only a unique and periodic attraction for purposes of material fertility; but an unbounded and continuous possibility of contact between minds rather than bodies; the play of countless subtle antennae seeking one another in the light and darkness of the soul; the pull towards mutual sensibility and completion, in which preoccupation with pre-

33

serving the species gradually dissolves in the greater intoxication of two people creating a world. It is fact, that through woman the universe advances towards man. The whole question (the vital question for the earth) is that they shall recognize one another.

If man fails to recognize the true nature, the true object of his love the confusion is vast and irremediable. Bent on assuaging a passion intended for the All on an object too small to satisfy it, he will strive to compensate a fundamental imbalance by materialism or an ever increasing multiplicity of experiments. His efforts will be fruitless—and in the eyes of one who can see the inestimable value of the 'spiritual quantum' of man, a terrible waste. But let us put aside any sentimental feelings or virtuous indignation. Let us look very coolly, as biologists or engineers, at the lurid atmosphere of our great towns at evening. There and everywhere else as well, the earth is continually dissipating its most marvellous power. This is pure loss. Earth is burning away, wasted on the empty air. How much energy do you think the spirit of the earth loses in a single night?

If only man would turn and see the reality of the universe shining in the spirit and through the flesh. He would then discover the reason for what has hitherto deceived and perverted his powers of love. Woman stands before him as the lure and symbol of the world. He cannot embrace her except by himself growing, in his turn, to a world scale. And because the world is always growing and always unfinished and always ahead of us, to achieve his love man is engaged in a limitless conquest of the universe and himself. In this sense, man can only attain woman by consummating a union with the universe. Love is a sacred reserve of energy; it is like the blood of spiritual evolution. This is the first revelation we receive from the sense of the earth.

b Human Unity. In strange opposition to the irresistible attraction manifested in love is the instinctive repulsion which habitually drives human molecules apart. Independent of polarization that

brings the opposite sexes together, the individual seems in forming himself to isolate and close in on himself. Man, allegedly a
social being, feels at ease with any jungle creature. He somehow
bristles at the appearance of another man like himself. This reaction might at first sight seem to support the pluralists who see
the purpose of life as a dispersion of monads. In fact it can only
imply a nervousness or cowardice of the individual faced with a
task of expanding which would bring him liberation. In fact,
if what we have just said is true (at least as a whole)—that is to say,
if there is really a spirit of the earth in process of formation—then
the elements of that spirit would positively be unable to repel
one another. Indeed they must be concealing from one another
a fundamental attraction more powerful than any tendency to
mutual independence. This attraction is still dormant, it is true.
But are there not signs by which we can detect its presence?

Instinctively and in principle, man normally keeps his distance
from man. But on the other hand, how his powers increase if, in
research or competition, he feels the breath of affection or comradeship! What fulfilment when, at certain moments of enthusiasm or danger, he finds himself suddenly admitted to the
miracle of a common soul. These pale or brief illuminations should
give us a glimmering of the mighty power of joy and action that
is still within the human layer. Far from suspecting it, men suffer
and vegetate in their isolation; they need the intervention of a
higher impulse, to force them beyond the dead point at which
they are halted and propel them into the region of their deep
affinity. The sense of the earth is the irresistible pressure which
comes at a given moment to unite them in a common enthusiasm. Still lost in a crowd of their kind, men turn away from a
plurality which disturbs them. They cannot love millions of
strangers. By revealing to each one that a part of himself exists in
all the rest, the sense of the earth is now bringing into sight a new
principle of universal affection among the mass of living beings:
the devoted liking of one element for another within a single
world *in progress.*

In love, as we have already said, the attraction of the centre for all convergent beings takes shape and is felt. We are now discovering the possibility and glimpsing the outline of *a second fundamental affective component of the world*: the love of mutual linkage above the love of attraction, elements drawing together to achieve union. We already know a little about the second of these two passions. But who can express the still almost unknown qualitative fulfilment—the vast intoxication of brotherly friendship—which would accompany the victory over internal, residual multiplicity? Consciousness of human unity would at last be achieved. And what a force would accrue to the noosphere, not only for pity and mercy, but *for attack*!

c Scientific Research. The sense of the earth comes to give men the reason for their superabundance of love, and to show its possible use. It tends to break the disastrous isolation which envelops spiritual monads at their birth. At the same time it reveals itself as the force destined to set in motion and organize the crushing mass of human productions and discoveries. This is the next subject for us to consider.

For some hundreds of centuries—up to our own day, in fact—men did not create much more than their immediate, individual needs required. The greatest discoveries, such as fire, art, agriculture, trade and geometry, were not pushed beyond what was necessary for the support of the family or city; they behaved like good children, energies harnessed for domestic use. The individual in fact did not distinctly see any tangible reality above himself.

Today, after a rapid shift of balance which occurred without our seeing it, we are beginning to perceive that individual man has become to some extent subordinate to his work. Not only the machine, the field and gold, but things at first considered mere luxuries or simple curiosities (such as the means of rapid transport or research laboratories) have become a kind of autonomous entities, endowed with unbounded and exacting life. And the most disquieting thing—the only disquieting thing, should

36

one say?—is that this proliferation seems to take place without order, like a tissue that proliferates to the point of choking with its neoplasm the organism on which it was produced. From the economic and industrial point of view the crisis is evident. But it rages just as much in intellectual spheres, and affects the human mass itself. Too much iron, too much wheat, too many automobiles—but also too many books, too many observations; and also too many diplomas, technicians and workmen—and even too many children. The world cannot function without producing living beings, food, ideas. But its production is more and more patently exceeding its powers of absorption and assimilation. Here again, as in the case of love, we must ask what this excess production means. Is the world condemned, as it grows, to automatic death by stifling beneath its own excessive weight?

Not at all, we would answer. It is in course of gathering to itself a new and higher body. At this crisis of birth, everything depends on the prompt emergence of a soul which by merely appearing will come to organize, lighten and vitalize this mass of stagnant and confused matter. Now this soul, if it exists, can only be the 'conspiration' of individuals, associating to *raise* the edifice of life *to a new stage*. The resources at our disposal today, the powers that we have released, *could not possibly be absorbed* by the narrow system of individual or national units which the architects of the human earth have hitherto used. Our plan was to build a *big house*, larger but similar in design to our good old dwelling places. And now we have been led by the higher logic of progress which is in us, to collect components that are too big for the use we intended to make of them. *The age of nations has passed. Now, unless we wish to perish we must shake off our old prejudices and build the earth.* I know the kind of smiles that are exchanged when someone dares to suggest that man is confronted in the immediate future with the possibility of something new and greater than himself: the smile of the sceptic and the dilettante, the scribe and the pharisee. The more scientifically I regard the world, *the less can I see any possible biological future for it except the active consciousness of its unity.* Life cannot henceforth advance on our planet (and *nothing* will prevent its advancing—not even its inner servitudes) except by breaking down the partitions which still divide human activity and entrusting itself unhesitatingly to faith in the future.

There cannot be any growth for any division of the earth outside the progress of the earth itself. Let us place in the *forefront* of our concrete concerns a systematic organization and exploration of our universe, only considered as the true fatherland of humanity. Then, quite naturally, accumulated riches will regain motion, which is their soul; material energy will circulate and, more important still, spiritual energy, corrupted by the petty jealousies of present day society, will find its natural outlet in an attack on the mysteries of the world. Research has for long been considered by men an accessory, an eccentricity or a danger. The moment is approaching when we shall perceive that it is the highest of human functions. It will absorb the spirit of war and shine with the light of religions. To exert constant pressure on the whole area of reality, is this not the supreme sign of faith in Being, and therefore of worship? All this is ours if we learn not to stifle the spirit of earth in us.

But let there be no mistake. He who wishes to share in this spirit must die and be reborn, to himself and to others. To reach this higher plane of humanity, he must not only reflect and see a particular situation intellectually, but make a complete change in his fundamental way of valuation and action. In him, *a new plane* (individual, social and religious) *must eliminate another.* This entails inner tortures and persecutions. *The earth will only become conscious of itself through the crisis of conversion.*

V THE FUTURE OF THE SPIRIT

And now that we have hypothetically reversed our habitual thought in two respects—first seeing that spirit has more consistence than matter in the universe; and then that life on earth is in some ways more interesting and real than lives—we discover to our surprise a question so vast and concrete confronting us that we cannot understand how the majority of human beings are not more generally impressed by it. How solid in fact are the things we have built? Where is our civilization going? Is not the noosphere implacably condemned from birth to wither and disappear on account of the limited and precarious basis afforded it by our planet? *What is the future of the spirit of the earth?*

There was a time when the earth still appeared large, almost boundless. Its bottom touched hell, and its highest peaks held converse with the heavens. Until last century it was a great business to travel to the antipodes. Over the poles and within the great continents floated a bright cloud of mystery. We have seen this heroic and fascinating period of exploration concluded in a few years. The human tide has covered everything. The earth is once and for all encircled by spirit. And with the constantly accelerated progress of aerial or etheric means of communication, it is shrinking beneath our eyes to a ludicrously small domain. In step with this most rapid and impressive geographical diminution, the world is noticeably becoming exhausted in other ways by our continual scientific investigation. Of course whole departments of research are being discovered or revived. But others are becoming impoverished by intensive exploitation (the historical or descriptive sciences in particular). There will be no need to wait for sudden cataclysms or a slow change of physical conditions to make life on its surface impossible. The earth will surely become an uninhabitable prison for lack of power to stimulate and nourish the work of the mind.

Faced with these prospects which, I repeat, thanks to the growing speed of events, have left the realm of dreams and are beginning to take shape on our horizon as a precise eventuality, the first requisite is to make sure of an unshakable basis for our faith in the value of the world. It is patently very difficult (and somewhat futile) to attempt a guess at the condition of the world at the end of another geological period. But one point at least seems capable of being established by *analysis of the present facts*; and this is that unless we make up our minds to admit that the cosmos is intrinsically an absurdity, the growth of the spirit must be taken as irreversible. 'The spirit *as a whole* will never fall back.' In other words 'In an evolutionary universe, the existence of spirit by its nature rules out the possibility of a death in which the achievements of the spirit will *totally* disappear or to be more precise, in which they will not survive in *the form of their flowering*.' Such is the infinitely comforting guarantee afforded us by these few words which express a stroke of immediate and fundamental intuition: 'The world would justifiably and infallibly cease to act—out of discouragement—if it became aware (in its thinking zones) that it is going to a total death. Therefore *total death does not exist*.'

This argument will, I know, appear suspect to many. Many thinkers, after the example of H. Poincaré, accepting a fashionable agnosticism or seduced by the false lure of stoicism or a very fine altruism, believe that they can accept without weakening the idea that thought on earth will last only a moment, and that we must devote everything to that moment, which is a' lightning-flash in the night'. These thinkers have, I believe, deluded themselves by not following to its conclusion the significance of this phrase: *total death* of the universe. Unconsciously, I am certain, they stop short of finding the full meaning of the words they use. They are assuming that some trace of this 'lightning-flash' will remain; something will be preserved by a consciousness, a memory, a glance. But even this last hope must be abandoned if the idea of absolute death (probably as absurd as the idea of nothingness) is to be given its full force. No, not even a trace. (It would still mean everything to the universe even for an instant to have cast its spell on an observer who will retain that vision for ever!) Around us total, impenetrable darkness, which will let *nothing* of all we have understood and achieved filter through to *anyone*. Then why make efforts? Why follow the orders and expectations of evolution? Out of supreme altruism? But there is no virtue in sacrifice when no higher interest is at stake. A universe which would continue *to act laboriously* in the conscious expectation of absolute death would be a stupid world, a spiritual monstrosity, in fact a chimera. Now since in fact the world appears before us here and now as one huge action perpetually taking place with formidable assurance, there can be no doubt at all that it is capable of nourishing indefinitely in its offspring an appetite for life, which is continually growing more critical, exacting and refined. It must carry within it the guarantees of ultimate success. From the moment that it admits thought, a universe can no longer be simply temporary or of limited evolution: it must by its very structure emerge into the absolute.[1] Consequently, however unstable life may appear, however impressive its connexions with limiting space and forces of disintegration, one thing above all is certain (because it is as certain as the world!): spirit will always succeed, as it has done till now, in defying risks and determinisms. It is the indestructible part of the universe.[2]

[1]There can be nothing more typical or more distressing than the description offered by the great English astronomer Sir James Jeans, in his last and widely read book, *The Universe around Us*, of the future state of the world in 'a million million years'; a humanity presumed to be like ours growing old without hope of any morrow on an earth without peaks or mysteries. Jeans offers us this prospect as a 'hope', since we have still a long life in front of us (as if our appetite for life, faced by *absolute and certain death*, would find any difference between one year and a million million!). Strange that he can have so little understood both the human spirit's reserves of power and its requirements.

[2]'At first, we could only note with astonishment, but not explain the persistent rise of a fraction of the world, against the current, towards ever more improbable states of complexity. Now we understand that this paradoxical movement is sustained by a prime mover ahead . . . From this point of view . . . evolution assumes its true figure for our mind and our heart. It is certainly not "creative", as science for a brief moment believed; but it is the expression of creation, for our experience, in time and space.' ('Man's Place in the Universe' in *The Vision of the Past*, p. 231.)

Let us now return to the earth itself and try to guess what the further periods of its spiritual evolution will be.

In the course of a first phase, one may legitimately suppose that the narrow limits to which it confines us, far from being a cause of weakness, represent on the contrary a necessary condition of progress. There is, as we have already pointed out, a spirit of the earth. But in order to take form and shape, this spirit needs a powerful concentrating agent to bring men together and increase their powers of acting as a crowd. We can already see before our eyes the first coming together of the human layer taking place in the form of an interpenetration of thoughts and interests. No similar effect would be possible in an inhabited field without limits. Let us extend, in thought, this process of continuous unification, in the course of which the inner affinities of the elements are forced together by the very form of the planet on which we dwell. What new power may not issue from this drastic treatment of 'spiritual matter'? It pains us to be thus forced into a mould, since our liberties are momentarily hampered and because, certain material links being (perhaps inevitably) *in advance* in this task of 'soul-making', we feel ourselves to be coming to the state of the machine and the termite colony. But let us put our trust in spiritual energies. True union does not stifle or confuse its elements; it super-differentiates them in unity. A little more time and the spirit of the earth will emerge from this ordeal with its specific individuality, its own character and features. And then, on the surface of the noosphere, gradually elevated in its preoccupations and passions—always reaching out to solve higher problems and possess greater objects—*the striving for being will reach its maximum.*

When this stage is passed, there comes the great puzzle. What will happen at the critical period when life on earth becomes mature? Shall we at that moment be capable of joining with other centres of cosmic life to resume the work of universal synthesis on a higher scale? Or shall we, without leaving the earth, penetrate some new surface of ontological discontinuity—vitalization, hominization and then a third stage? Most probably the third event will take place. But this can only be glimpsed if we bring into account the spiritual influence of God.

VI THE ARISING OF GOD

Contemporary man has passed through a period of great illusion in imagining that, having attained a better knowledge of himself and the world, he has no more need of religion. The result of the two great modern discoveries of space and time, culminating in the knowledge of evolution, has undoubtedly been to produce many detailed schematizations. It may consequently have seemed (at least for a moment) that nothing of our past beliefs remained. Indeed there have been a great number of systems in which the fact of religion was interpreted as a psychological phenomenon linked with the childhood of humanity. At its greatest, at the origins of civilization, it had gradually to decline and give place to more positive theories from which God (a personal and transcendent God above all) must be excluded. This was a pure illusion. In reality, for anyone who can see, the great conflict from which we have just emerged has merely strengthened the world's need for belief. Having reached a higher stage in self-mastery, the spirit of the earth is discovering a more and more vital need to worship; *from universal evolution God emerges* in our minds greater and more necessary than ever.

Let us briefly sketch, now that we are able to understand them a little better, the great phases of this continuous arising of God (looking below the veil and details of the great religions).

The birth and progress of the idea of God on earth are intimately bound up with the phenomenon of hominization. At the very moment when life reflects on itself—by virtue of that same movement—it finds itself facing *the problem of action*. It becomes awake to itself on the ascending and difficult road of progressive unification. How will it explain to itself this primal and congenital

43

duty? Where will it find not only the authority but the courage and desire for this effort? We have briefly set out, a few lines back, an outline of the only possible answer to this question which life asks itself. No consideration should, rightly speaking, decide us to take a single step forward without a knowledge that the ascending path leads to *a peak from which life will never descend again*. The sole possible instigator of reflective life must therefore be an absolute, that is to say a divine goal. Religion can become an opium. It is too often understood as a simple soothing of our woes. *Its true function is to sustain and spur on the progress of life.* We are far from wishing to imply that from its beginnings this conviction stood out in the human mind as clearly as it does for us today. But we can recognize now that, underlying much simpler and more childish interpretations, there was really this profound need for an absolute. Beneath all the progressive forms of religion, it is the absolute that was sought.

Now once we have established this point of departure, it becomes clear that the 'religious function', born of hominization and linked with it, cannot but grow continuously with man himself. Contrary to the beliefs of many, the more man becomes himself the more he feels the need to devote himself to one greater than he. Is not this a fact that we can observe all around us? At what moment has there been a more urgent need in the noosphere to find a faith and hope in order to give sense and a soul to the immense organism we are constructing? Has the struggle ever been more violent between love and hatred of life? We waver today between two desires: to serve the world and go on strike. Since life cannot possibly perish or, therefore, revolt against itself, we must be very close to the open triumph of adoration!

And indeed, step by step with the growing expectation of humanity, the face of God seems gradually to loom larger through the world. God has sometimes seemed to disappear, eclipsed by the organic vastness of the cosmos that was being revealed to us. Once we understand that the universe is supported solely by the future and the spirit, these new immensities cannot fail to reveal to us the majesty, the grandeur and the overpowering richness of the summit towards which all things converge. Gladly, the 'unbelievers' of our time bow before the 'god energy'. But it is impossible to stop at this somewhat vague stage of materialistic pantheism. Under penalty of being less evolved than the ends brought about by its own action *universal energy must be a thinking energy*. Consequently, as we shall see, the attributes of cosmic value, with which it is irradiated to our modern eyes, in no way abolish our need to recognize it as a transcendent *form of personality*.

The personality of God (together with the survival of the 'soul') calls out the greatest opposition and antipathy from contemporary scientific thought. The origin of this dislike is to be found in the intellectual contempt which has rejected as 'anthropocentric' all attempts to understand the universe through man. Let us once more put the fact of man in its true place. Let us recognize, not out of vanity or idleness but on scientific evidence, that no phenomenon has had more preparation, or is more axial and characteristic than this. And at the same time we are compelled to admit that even (and particularly) today, because of the new value man is assuming in nature, the idea of a God conceived as a distinct and animate centre of the world is necessarily in full growth. Let us say, in fact, substituting one equivalent formula for another, that by the capital event of *hominization*, the most advanced portion of the cosmos has become *personalized*. This simple change of variable brings in sight, for the future, a double condition of existence which is quite inevitable.

First of all, since everything *in the universe beyond man* takes place within *personalized being*, the final divine term of universal convergence must also (eminently) possess the quality of a person (without which it would be inferior to the elements it governs). But there is a further observation to be made, a little subtler but no less certain. To the idea of a personal (or rather super-personal) centre emerging from multiplicity, we at first react by imagining this centre as forming itself from the legacy or 'remains' of inferior centres of personality which surrender their progress to it. Now this is an inaccurate view, and arises from the fact that we transfer unaltered into *the personalized sphere of the world* a type of heredity peculiar to infra-personal zones of the cosmos. Let us reflect further, and we shall recognize that a *person* can only transmit (and can only have the vital desire to transmit) *its own personality* to evolution. We imagine that by the progress of cosmic being, this person becomes 'super-centred', or centred not on itself but on a higher being. But it would not be possible for it to pass to this centre as a gift presented by itself, *which would not be itself*. For its whole quality lies in *being itself*—the incommunicable expression of a conscious observation point upon the universe. If this is the case, the final summit of the perfected—that is to say personalized—world (that is to say God) can in no way be conceived as born of a sort of aggregation of elementary personalities (since these are, by nature, irremovable from their own centres). In order to *super-animate without destroying* a universe formed of personal elements, it must be a special centre itself. In this way traditional conceptions of a god exerting intellectual influence on immortal monads distinct from him reappear, no longer sentimental and instinctive but closely linked to contemporary evolutionary ideas (provided that man is not excluded from them).

And now all that has been said in these pages concerning the spirit of the earth must, to be completed, be supplemented by another view. We have followed the cosmic spiritual phenomenon *from within* by the path of simple immanence. But now by logic of this path itself, we are forced to turn and to recognize that the current which elevates matter must be conceived rather as a *tide* than as a simple internal pressure. Multiplicity ascends attracted and engulfed by something which is 'already one'. This is the secret and guarantee of the irreversibility of life.

In an initial phase—before man—the attraction was vitally but blindly received by the world. Since man's coming, it has become at least partially conscious in the form of reflective freedom, and it has given rise to religion. Religion is not a strictly individual crisis—or choice or intuition—but represents the long disclosure of God's being through the collective experience of the whole of humanity, God reflecting himself personally on the organized sum of thinking monads to guarantee an assured success and fix precise laws for their hesitant activities. God bent over the now intelligent mirror of earth to impress on it the first marks of his beauty.

The last phase of this vast revelation, whose history is one with that of the world, cannot be other than the history of union, which will take place when the attraction of God, victorious over the material resistances caused by unorganized plurality, will once and for all have rescued from inferior determinisms the spirit slowly nourished by all the sap of the earth.

How will the spiritual evolution of our planet end, we asked at the conclusion of the preceding chapter? Perhaps, we will now reply, in a psychic rather than material turning about—possibly like a death—which will in fact be a liberation from the material plane of history and elevation in God.

Unpublished, The Pacific, 9 March, 1931.

THE SIGNIFICANCE AND POSITIVE
VALUE OF SUFFERING

Illness naturally tends to give sufferers the feeling that they are useless or even a burden on the earth. Almost inevitably they feel as if cast up by the great stream of life, lying by sheer ill-luck incapable of work or activity. Their state seems to have no meaning. It reduces them, they might say, to inaction amidst a universe in action.

The following observations are designed to help dissipate these depressing views by showing, from a hypothetical standpoint, the place and use of suffering in the construction even of the visible world.

I THE CONSTRUCTION OF THE WORLD

In the first place the world is under construction. This is a fundamental truth which must be understood at the start, and so thoroughly understood as to become habitual and more or less natural to our thought. At first sight, beings and their fate may possibly appear to be distributed by chance, or at least arbitrarily, over the face of the earth. We are within an ace of thinking that each one of us might have been born indifferently earlier or later, here or there, more or less fortunate. The universe from the beginning to the end of its history might seem like a sort of vast flower-bed in time and space in which the flowers are interchangeable at the gardener's whim. This view seems at fault. The more we reflect, making use of what we have learnt from science, philosophy and religion, each along its own lines, the more we see that the world must be compared not to a bundle of elements in artificial juxtaposition but to an organized system, informed by a broad unity of growth proper to itself. Through the centuries, a general plan appears truly to be in course of realization around us. Something is afoot in the universe, a result is working out which can best be compared to a gestation and birth: the birth of a spiritual reality formed by souls and the matter they draw after them. Laboriously, by way of human activity and thanks to it, the new earth is gathering, isolating and purifying itself. No, we are not like flowers in a bunch, but the leaves and flowers of a great tree, on which each appears at its time and place, according to the demands of the All.

II THE SIGNIFICANCE OF SUFFERING

This conception of a world in the state of growth might seem ingenious but abstract. In fact it has important practical consequences. For it leads to nothing less than the renewal in our minds of the idea we have ourselves formed either of the value of personal human effort (which increases with the whole work of the universe of which it is part) or (and it is only this that interests us here) of the value of individual human pain. Let us explain this last point a little, by returning to the comparison of the bunch of flowers and the tree.

In a bunch one would be surprised to see imperfect or 'sickly' flowers because the constituents have been gathered one by one, and artificially put together. On a tree, on the other hand, which has had to fight against inner accidents in its development and the external accidents of bad weather, broken branches, torn leaves, parched, sickly or wilted flowers are 'in place': they express the more or less difficult conditions of growth encountered by the trunk that bears them.

Similarly, in a universe where each creature forms a little

whole enclosed and desired for its own sake and theoretically transposable at will, we should have some difficulty in mentally justifying the presence of individuals sadly arrested in their possibilities of ascent. Why this arbitrary inequality, these gratuitous restrictions? On the other hand, if the world in fact represents a work of achievement at present taking place; if at birth we are really thrown into the midst of a battle, we can see that, for the success of the universal effort of which we are at the same time the participators and the stake, it is inevitable that there shall be pain. The world, seen by experience at our level, is an immense groping, an immense search, an immense attack; its progress can take place only at the expense of many failures, of many wounds. Sufferers of whatever species are the expression of this stern but noble condition. They are not useless and dwarfed. They are simply paying for the forward march and triumph of all. They are casualties, fallen on the field of honour.

III THE POSITIVE VALUE OF SUFFERING

Let us go a little further. In the collective man formed by all men together and subordinated to Christ within the 'mystical body', there are, as St. Paul has told us, different organs and functions. What part can we imagine to be more specially entrusted with the task of sublimating and spiritualizing the general work of progress and conquest? The contemplatives and prayerful no doubt. But also, most certainly, the sick and suffering. By nature and temperament sufferers are in a sense driven out of themselves, compelled to depart from the prevailing forms of life. Are they not therefore by this very fact destined and chosen for the task of raising the world above immediate enjoyment towards an ever higher light? It is for them to stretch up to the divine more deliberately and more purely than the rest. It is for them to bring aid to their brothers who are working like miners in the bowels of matter. Thus it is those who bear in their weakened bodies the weight of the world in motion that by providential compensation prove the most active agents in the very progress that seems to be sacrificing and breaking them.

IV THE CONSEQUENT 'CONVERSION' OF THE WORLD'S SUFFERING

If these remarks are true, the sick man in his apparent inactivity has a very grand human task to fulfil. He must of course never cease to aim at his own cure and recovery. Also he must of course use all the strength that remains to him for the different kinds of sometimes extremely productive work that are within his powers. Christian resignation, in fact, is just the opposite of giving up. Once he has resolved to combat his sickness in this way, the sick man must realize that in proportion to his sickness he has a special function to perform, in which no one can replace him: the task of co-operating in the transformation (one might say conversion) of human suffering.

What a vast ocean of human suffering spreads over the entire earth at every moment! Of what is this mass formed? Of blackness, gaps and rejections? No, let me repeat, of potential energy. In suffering the ascending force of the world is concealed in a very intense form. The whole question is how to liberate it and give it a consciousness of its significance and potentialities. The world would leap high towards God if all the sick together were to turn their pain into a common desire that the kingdom of God should come to rapid fruition through the conquest and organization of the earth. All the sufferers of the earth joining their sufferings so that the world's pain might become a great and unique act of consciousness, elevation and union. Would not this be one of the highest forms that the mysterious work of creation could take in our sight?

Could it not be precisely for this that the creation was completed in Christian eyes by the passion of Jesus? On the cross, we are perhaps in danger of seeing only an individual suffering, a single act of expiation. The creative power of that death escapes us. Let us take a broader glance, and we shall see that the cross is the symbol and place of an action whose intensity is beyond expression. Even from the earthly point of view, the crucified Jesus, fully understood, is not rejected or conquered. It is on the contrary he who bears the weight and draws ever higher towards God the universal march of progress. Let us act like him, in order to be in our whole existence united with him.

From *Trait d'Union*, the organ of *L'Union catholique des Malades*, 1 April, 1933.

SKETCH OF A PERSONALISTIC UNIVERSE

It may seem that the world of collective human thought has reached a sort of dead end in its efforts towards understanding. The advance-guard of science has long ago agreed to recognize that we live in an evolutionary universe. In front and behind us all realities multiply indefinitely. Nobody whose thought is of importance any longer doubts that this incessant becoming is one of the most objective and general conditions of experience.

But has this becoming a direction? Is this evolution directed? Here scientists, in all sincerity, hesitate. Like hounds that have lost the scent, they circle but advance no further, or even decide to give up the chase. 'No, we are probably going nowhere. Or if we are going anywhere it is impossible for us to guess where since we have no points of reference. Everything is in movement and nothing advances.' This is the opinion of a good half of the most intelligent men of my acquaintance.

The following pages are an attempt to cross the barrier without undue recourse to any philosophy. We are confronting one of nature's problems to discover the direction of evolution, if there is one. We must solve it without leaving the realm of scientific facts. And this is what I shall try to do here.

As a point of departure for this attempt, I choose once more the

[1] To avoid any misunderstanding, Teilhard glossed the French title of this little work in English, 'A Personalistic Universe', as above. (*Ed.*)

hypothesis strongly indicated by the findings of biology, that consciousness has continuously grown through living beings, and that the reflective, personal form that it has attained in man is the most characteristic that we know. By this, I must state once more, I am introducing no judgement of absolute value. I do not seek to know whether a more conscious being is *absolutely* better than a less conscious one. I confine myself to recording that more conscious matter (that is to say more reflective, better centred) follows historically after less centred, less reflective, less conscious. This seems to be the work of 'a wind of the spirit', to be observed throughout the world. How can we definitely establish this fact which, if proved, would also give us the proof we seek of a definite movement of the universe?

I would answer by accepting it and by enquiring whether, pushed to its final conclusions, it gives a true picture of the universe around us. The physical sciences know no other criterion than this conformity to their actual development.

What I ultimately propose therefore in this essay is to construct a picture of the physical world around the human personality chosen as an element to stand for the whole system. Once we admit that the reflective monad represents *the mesh* of the cosmos, what structure and what future are we led to attribute to it? This is what I shall try to discover.

On my way, I shall concern myself only to pursue to their logical end the organic links which appear—just to see where they lead—rather as if I were constructing a geometrical system. The overall success will decide. If the construction does not form a complete whole, or if it contradicts some part of experience, it will show that the initial hypothesis was bad and should be abandoned. But if, on the contrary, it seems to encircle and harmonize the world to a greater degree, then we must conclude that in accepting a spiritual direction of evolution we have come near to the truth.

The *truth* is nothing but the total coherence of the universe in relation to each part of itself. Why suspect or undervalue this coherence because we are ourselves the observers? Scientists are always contrasting something they call anthropocentric illusion with something they call objective reality. The distinction does not exist. The truth of man is the truth of the universe for man, that is to say the truth, pure and simple.

'Don't chat, but try.'[1] Let us leave vain discussion and enquire as true positivists whether the universe is coherent in its elements and in the mass, when we try to extend it along the line of growing personalization, in the direction pointed by the human spearhead.

II THE FORMATION OF THE INDIVIDUAL

One first advantage that appears when one analyses and then constructs the cosmos by means of the human personality as our chosen element, is that its past immediately takes natural shape. Whenever one stands in the landscape one sees objects spread radially around one. But the observer also finds certain special points from which a certain organization of features, supposing one to exist, stands out with special clarity; a meeting of paths in a well-planted forest, the axis of a fold in a range of mountains. From any other point all is confusion. From such a point everything becomes clear. The general lines of the universe stand out and fall into groups if looked at from the position of the thinking being with whom we naturally coincide. Not only from man, as from any living being taken as a starting point, do the elements of the world distribute themselves concentrically (this being an essential property of time and space); but around man also these elements display a concentric structure, which can only occur at a nodal point in the universe.

This is indeed the viewpoint gradually imposed on us by the methodical distribution, on the various planes and azimuths of the past, of the beings which preceded us. Just as the powdering

[1] In English in the original text.

of stars, exactly placed on the vault of heaven, today takes in astronomers' eyes the form of immense spirals in motion, so the myriads of beings that we call life tend to arrange themselves according to a very simple law of psychic concentration, ending at the present moment of the world with man. Departing from man and descending towards origins, consciousness appears to grow slack and diffuse, and finally to become unidentifiable. Towards man, as we ascend the axis of time, spontaneity awakes, organizes itself, and finally reflects on itself by emerging into 'personality'.

I will not describe this process again; its accuracy, though many still dispute it (seemingly out of pure mechanistic habit), seems to me as evident as the majority of great hypotheses currently accepted by modern science. What applies directly to my subject is to discover the implications of this experimental fact for the ground texture of the *stuff of the universe*.

At a first analysis the condensation of cosmic reality into human personality seems to reveal a law of universal formation. For perfectly legitimate reasons of utility and method, the physical sciences have principally set out to trace phenomena in the direction of decomposition or atomization. The fact of evolution comes to remind us that the principal movement of reality is a synthesis, in the course of which plurality manifests itself in increasingly complex and organic forms, each further degree of unification being accompanied by a growth of inner consciousness and freedom. Within pure duration, undifferentiated and inert multiplicity does not exist. There are no doubt, in a secondary sense, dead ashes. But in itself, at the beginning, dust, in all its degrees, is an index of life at its birth. A first multiple is followed by a first unification; and at every successive stage of consciousness a new plurality is constituted to form a higher synthesis. Thus we may express the law of recurrence by which we are governed.

To express this general condition of our knowledge in another way, we might say that the universe appears to be affected by a convergent curvature into which the substance of all things is gradually forced. But in order to understand the precise nature of this curvature of our surroundings, it is necessary to start with ourselves and examine the significance of the law of universal concentration when applied to the analysis of our own personality. Since the arising of thought, men have continually wondered and argued about the coexistence and contradictions of spirit and matter. Plurality and unity: the single problem to which all the physical sciences, all philosophy and all religion fundamentally bring us back. We seem at the present day to be moving towards a solution: as always, when confronted with the most tiresome paradoxes (like that of liberty), we are forced to recognize that the question was badly framed, and that the problem does not exist. No contradiction in fact between the one and the many, if one regards things as existing in a flux of personalization; but simply two phases (or to be more exact two directions) in the same reality moving around us. Spirit and matter are contradictory if isolated and symbolized in the form of abstract, fixed notions of pure plurality and pure simplicity, which can in any case never be realized. '*In natura rerum*' one is inseparable from the other; one is never without the other; and this for the good reason that one appears essentially as a sequel to the synthesis of the other. No spirit (not even God within the limits of our experience) exists, nor could structurally exist without an associated multiple, any more than a centre without its circle or circumference. In a concrete sense there is not matter and spirit. All that exists is matter becoming spirit.[1] There is neither spirit nor matter in the world;

[1]To avoid all misunderstanding, it must not be forgotten that the author takes up his position on the plane of appearances—regarding the universe as it appears to us—and not on the ontological plane. He makes this clear in more than one place (for example on pp. 161-2) in this book: 'Understood in this way, let us observe, the conservation of personality in no way implies (quite the contrary) an "ontological" identity between the unconscious and the self-conscious. Although subjected to a "quantic" law, personalization remains in effect essentially an evolutionary transformation, that is to say continually the generator of something entirely new. "So much matter is needed for so much spirit; so much multiplicity for so much unity. Nothing is lost, yet everything is created." This is all that is affirmed.' (*Ed.*)

the 'stuff of the universe' is *spirit-matter*. No other substance but this could produce the human molecule.

I know very well that this idea of spirit-matter is regarded as a hybrid monster, a verbal exorcism of a duality which remains unresolved in its terms. But I remain convinced that the objections made to it arise from the mere fact that few people can make up their minds to abandon an old point of view and take the risk of a new idea. The early geometricians objected to the idea of incommensurables, because reality seemed to them inevitably to imply measurable quantities. Biologists or philosophers cannot conceive a biosphere or noosphere because they are unwilling to abandon a certain narrow conception of individuality.

Nevertheless the step must be taken. For in fact pure spirituality is as inconceivable as pure materiality. Just as, in a sense, there is no geometrical point, but as many structurally different points as there are methods of deriving them from different figures (centre of a sphere, apex of a cone, focal points of an ellipse, etc.) so every spirit derives its reality and nature from a particular type of universal synthesis. Whatever its 'purity', however great its purity, it is the crown and expression of a genesis. The 'higher' a being is in duration, the greater and more finely unified the complexity that it contains in its solid parts. The reality of spirit-matter is inevitably translated into and confirmed by a *structure of the spirit*.[1]

Structure does not imply *corruptibility*. The impossible notion of 'pure spirit' seems to be born from the desire to make 'souls' safe from a death, which has seemed inevitably linked with *composition*. Now this is only another demonstration of the inability of all static figurations to express the universe. In an immobilist perspective, it is possible for the aggregation of elements in a unity necessarily to imply an eventual disaggregation of that unity. It is no longer the same in a cosmos envisaged as polarized on an ever increasing concentration of itself. However complex

[1] This structure could be said to be the 'nature' on which the 'personality' is centred.

such a cosmos may be, it cannot be decomposed so long as the arrow of time is not reversed. Incorruptibility no longer seems linked to simplicity, but simply to *irreversibility*.

That the personalization of the universe, having at this moment reached the human stage in ourselves, is irreversible we shall soon recognize, step by step, as the conditions of internal coherence peculiar to a personal universe yield to our analysis. In this way the 'inalterability' of the person, so rightly defended by spiritualist philosophies, will at the same time be preserved and attached to an intelligible physical theory.

Here for the dual purpose of preparing an element essential for this demonstration and providing a necessary complement for the preceding argument, we must add a final feature to the fundamental law of recurrence in which, like many others before us, we believe we can discern the true shape of the universe. For the world, as we have said, to advance in duration is to progress in physical concentration. The continuity of evolution is expressed in a movement of this kind. But in the course of this same continuity, discontinuities can and indeed must occur. For no psychical entity can, to our knowledge, grow indefinitely; always at a given moment it meets one of those critical points at which it changes state.

The human personality seems by its appearance on earth to mark one of these changes of state. Before it, so far as we can judge, there were in nature only 'rough sketches of personalities', or even, taking life in its most distant stages, rough sketches of individuals. Where in the plant or the polyp colony can we place its unity? It is so diffuse. And then gradually, as time goes on, attempts become regular. Associations of cells combine in more precise groups. Combined movements and reactions take shape. In the higher animals, psychism is already on the level of personality. And yet, even in the most 'intelligent' ape, one fundamental property is still lacking: the possibility of consciousness furling back on itself. Reflexion, the sudden and total transition from the diffuse to the single-pointed, marks and defines the coming of an absolutely new state of consciousness. With it, thought breaks into being and life, 'hominized' life, takes possession of the earth for a second time.

Before man, the slow maturing, by way of frail individualities, of a *state of personality*.

In man, by way of a critical point, the first appearance of unity, of the completed *personal molecule*.[1]

Here the teachings of history end for us. Now, if we wish to circle the whole horizon it is a question of turning towards the future. Personality has helped us to understand the structure of the world which bears and surrounds us. To what extent does it define the universe ahead of us?

---

[1]The act (of creative transformation or generalized evolution) is in itself *co-extensive* with the duration of the universe in growth, though one must naturally distinguish, along the whole curve followed by the being in its growth, certain stages, certain singular points.

'Creative transformation' varies in depth according to the height and novelty of the synthesis to be effected. It is in continuous play since the universe never ceases to grow (cosmogenesis). But a number of moments of stress can be distinguished at which it exercises itself more fully. The supreme case would be that of the creation of man. It cannot be said *baldly* that man as a special being born at his marked place in the universe was created complete out of nothing since—according to the letter of Genesis and the doctrine of evolution alike—the matter of his body was furnished by pre-existing elements. As for his spiritual soul, relatively independent of the body it inspires, it does not constitute a being on its own; as the *unifying* principle of the human being, it can only appear 'in the exercise of an act of union', that is to say, when acting on an object proportionate to it, this action consisting of 'unifying around it a universe which without it would lapse into plurality'.

In the view of Père Maréchal, quoted on p. 13, a conception of this sort is certainly acceptable not only to Catholic orthodoxy in general, but to Thomist philosophers also. (N. M. Wildiers.)

III EXTENSIONS OF THE PERSONALITY

Though the personal molecule, viewed backwards along the axis of time, is easily analysed into increasingly diffuse elements of personality, it seems at first sight to defy higher syntheses. In very virtue of its genesis by concentration, the spirit tends to close in on itself. The reflective stage at which consciousness comes to coincide with its own ground appears to mark thereafter for the mechanism of personalization a limit that cannot be passed. Can a centre centre itself outside itself?

All sorts of indications might lead one to suppose that with hominization the evolution of life has effectively reached the natural end of its progress on earth. The further the thinking individual advances in his own thought, the more impervious he apparently becomes to others. He is as if imprisoned in his own success. Man, by the very fact of his individualization, seems to become incapable of communication and incomprehensible to others around him. He then no longer sees any answer to the need for universal communion, which nevertheless exercises him, except in a turning back and unconscious re-immersion in the multitude:

> Lord, you have made me powerful and solitary,
> Let me fall asleep now in the sleep of the earth.[1]

A sort of crumbling, a granulation into monads neutralized as far as the others are concerned, this then would seem to be the transformation undergone by the stuff of the universe on reaching the last stage of its evolution. The torch of the universe is going out in and around us in a spatter of sparks. Evolution culminates in dispersion. Such is the thought of those who estimate existence solely by the value of the present moment, and on this they base their actions.

It is indisputable that the birth of reflective centres represents a

[1] Vigny, A. de, *Moïse*. The first line is slightly misquoted. (*Trans.*)

dangerous period for the life that engenders them. Out of intellectual giddiness, or intoxicated by their freedom, the personal molecules cannot escape the temptation of egoism, that is to say of independence. Isn't it wise to hang on to what one holds? Isn't it an essential duty to perfect within oneself the individuality entrusted to one? How can we possibly guess moreover whether there exists outside us a chance of surviving in a higher and more durable unity?

A cautious dispersion into autonomy or a still further convergence at all costs? Where lies the truth? To escape from this vital uncertainty in which evolution has been arrested within us, I can see no other means within the hypothesis in which these lines are written, but to analyse still further the texture of the being of which we are made. We are faced with an alternative. Either the fibres of the *Weltstoff* coil in on themselves within the human personality and 'have no way out'; and this means that we are really terminal cells, in which the cosmos is now due to break up. Or on the other hand, by way of the knot formed by our individuality, these same fibres extend and are destined to go further: and this would prove that by remaining true (that is to say coherent with the world) we must try to achieve all together some further synthesis.

The factual answer to this question does not seem in doubt. The lines of the universe do not bend back in closed curves within our being, but are held together as a sheaf within the unity of our ego only by their link with the future. This seems to me a fact established by the universal experience of humanity. If the world were ripe in our souls we should find equilibrium and rest in our completion. We should be able to be self-enclosed. Now the contrary is the case; we are constantly escaping from ourselves in our very effort to possess ourselves. What we love in the last resort in our personality is always 'another' ahead of us. We are incomplete, unfinished. There *must* therefore be a way out at the end of the blind alley in which the mechanism of personalization might seem to have confined us. Despite the antipathies with which it is riddled, the human mass is not a divergent plurality, but a multiple destined once more to undergo the synthesizing process of life. Structurally the universe certainly continues beyond ourselves. Evolution goes on, even after man. The whole of us does not die. But how can we conceive the possibility of this movement and how help it?

The solution of this problem is given by the very terms in which it is presented. By the process of our growth we find ourselves under the double necessity of deepening ourselves and simultaneously passing in some way into our surroundings. So, no doubt these two actions are not so opposed as they appear, but are linked in the harmony of a single underlying movement. Man avoids communication with another because he is afraid that by sharing he will diminish his personality. He seeks to grow by isolating himself. Now if the universe is organically possible (that is to say if it does not place us by birth in a mechanically impossible position) the very opposite is true. The gift we make of our being, far from threatening our ego, must have the effect of completing it.

This is the truth. Not only *a priori*, that is to say by deducing the future of the world from a property which conditioned its past; but *a posteriori* by observing around us the creative effects of love, we are led to accept this paradoxical proposition, which contains the final secret of life: true union does not fuse the elements it brings together, by mutual fertilization and adaptation it gives them a renewal of vitality. It is egoism that hardens and neutralizes the human stuff. *Union differentiates.*

Thus the law of fundamental convergence reappears not only below but above us as well. Union made us men by organizing the confused powers of matter under the control of a thinking spirit. It will now transform us into supermen by making us into elements governed by some higher soul. Up to now inner union has personalized us. Now external union is going to 'superpersonalize' us.

Now the significance and value of the groupings into which

what Marx called historical materialism is pushing us despite ourselves, are beginning to become plain. Left to their own impulses
(but for the case of sexuality) men would generally be much more
susceptible to mutual repulsion than to mutual attraction. To be
more themselves, they try prematurely to be alone. In opposition
to this separatist instinct, the necessities of life drive them into
society. Hence the manifold groupings, which become ever more
widespread and tyrannical, whose tentacles multiply and seize
us from all directions: political, economic, religious associations.
Caught in these bonds, we have the impression that our being is
about to disappear; we go through the anguish of being choked.
I shall have to speak again of this agony of the personality, and
enquire what conditions the socialization of the world must satisfy
if it is to save, not kill, the human cell. Here the important thing to
note is that if union truly superpersonalizes, the collective entities
whose birth and successive growths alarm us are *forming in the
foreseen direction of evolution*. They are the announcement, the
adumbration of a higher spirituality and therefore of a higher freedom. It is impossible to distinguish yet what, in this mass in full
transformation, is a monstrosity or what are final features or a
transitory stage. But one thing is certain: despite our fears, it is in
the direction of 'groupings' that we must advance.

The cause of our dislike of collectivity lies in the illusion which
makes us stubbornly identify 'personal' with 'individual'. This
confusion and the reactions it produces should disappear if the
fundamental law of being is really, as the physical sciences and
history teach us, that 'union differentiates'. By this rule we can
only attain our true ego and survive in it by organically associating ourselves with all the rest. What is legitimate and holy in our
egoism[1] must therefore contribute to the building of a universal
spirit in the depths of ourselves.

In analysing the *formation of the personality*, we have been led to
recognize the properties of a spirit-matter in the stuff of the uni-

[1]'Egoism' is clearly taken here in the sense of a non-injurious attachment to
self. (*Ed.*)

64

verse. Now another no less paradoxical aspect of this same stuff appears, revealed as necessary for any 'prolongation of the personality' beyond itself. I mean the *personal-universal*. The most incommunicable and therefore the most precious quality of each being is that which makes him one with all the rest. It is consequently by coinciding with all the rest that we shall find the centre of ourselves.

This new form assumed by the principle of convergence is richly productive. Not only does it define for us a route to be followed if we wish to remain faithful to the logic of the world in evolution. But it already makes clear the possibility and nature of what our consummation must be.

IV THE CONSUMMATION OF THE PERSONALITY

What prevents our consciousness from confining itself to our individual consciousness is, to be brief, the presence in ourselves of a plurality which is not reduced by hominization. In the system whose logic we have accepted, humanity is not the goal of the cosmos because it is still manifold. This means that by the sole fact that evolution passes through the human personality without staying there, we are forced to place the goal of this movement, which is drawing us on, infinitely further ahead. We imagined that striking land in ourselves we had reached the harbour. On the contrary we are launched back on the ocean of an immense future in which there is no possible stopping-place before the appearance of a single centre of the noosphere.[1]

Any attempt to imagine the concrete nature of such a far distant

[1]This theory allows us to envisage by way of stages some intermediate critical points, signalled by the appearance around us of higher souls which will engulf us but not destroy us (see our later remarks about the function of the universal centre). But in so far as these critical points lead only to the formation of another multiple, however reduced it may be, they can only mark stages of transition. The 'end of the world' is still further on.

reality would be entirely vain. To do so, we must already have reached the goal of the journey. But we must attempt here to express in our present scale of measurement the conditions which this end must satisfy to be capable of representation on our maps of the universe. How otherwise could we plan our route? Let us make an attempt.

By reason of the structure of the *Weltstoff* which we have already recognized, the first and also the most certain characteristic that we must expect in the final state of the universe is that it will be personal, with a personality so rich and with such control of itself that our souls can only be a frail model of it. The human monad is personal because centred. But there are infinite ways of being a centre, depending on the density of the convergent radii and the closeness of their connexion. In the completed universe, the richness and perfection of the synthesis being by hypothesis brought to their maximum, consciousness linked to this synthesis must perforce attain its highest degree. In the final shape assumed by the cosmos, personality, growing with convergence, must be at its greatest.

It has become a sort of principle of modern thought that the two attributes of totality and reflective consciousness cannot be associated in the same subject. The falsity of this postulate is proved by the ease with which the analysis of a world of convergent curvature has led us to the idea of the personal-universal. It is surely a 'pseudo-idea' that makes us think of a universe spread out in space and time. Totality can only be grasped at the point where it gathers. And such a point is perfectly conceivable since, in the realm of spirit-matter, nothing limits the inner complexity of a point.

So, starting from the human corpuscle, the extrapolation of the trajectory followed by the world can only lead us to the final stage of a personality of the universe. How can we define this supreme personality in relation to ourselves?

Here we must note the entirely special rules imposed on our reasonings (or rather on our calculations) by the introduction of dimensions of personality. Below man, we have little knowledge of what goes on in incompletely personalized beings. But we have the impression that at this level of evolution 'fusings of immanences' may take place. Two fragments of diffuse consciousness may, perhaps, add themselves together, to lose themselves in a third and higher consciousness; for what they have to transmit by this gift is not so much a soul as the particular state of animation that they have reached. Viable or not, in the deep levels of thought, this process of fusion appears definitely impossible once the stage of hominization has been passed. A person cannot disappear by passing into another person; for by nature he can only give himself *as a person* so long as he remains a self-conscious unity, that is to say *distinct*. Moreover, as we have seen, this gift which he makes of himself has the direct result of reinforcing his most incommunicable quality, that is to say the quality of superpersonalizing. 'Union differentiates.'

Let us apply these observations to the 'summation' of the universe in God—since God also is the name given by man to the consummated being.

God, as I have often remarked elsewhere, is almost inevitably conceived by a modern positivist as an ocean without shores, in which all things are totalized by loss of themselves. Our generation, essentially pantheist because evolutionist, seems to understand pantheism only in the form of a dissolution of individuals in a diffuse vastness. This is an illusion, caused by the fact that the unity of the world is wrongly sought, by influence of the physical sciences, in the direction of the increasingly simple energies into which it dissolves: *God is ether*, they would have said some years ago. A completely different result is obtained if one tries, as I have done here, to extend the universe in the direction of personality, that is to say of synthesis. Then God does not appear in the fanning out but in the concentration of the stuff of the universe; not as a centre of dissolution but a focus of personalization. *He is spirit*, and from this two things follow.

On the one hand his own *I* cannot be formed of an aggregation of inferior human or super-human 'I's' gathered together by Him, since, as we have just seen, these 'I's' are not additive. He must therefore possess his particular immanence. On the other hand, correlatively, the inferior 'I's in the course of their ascent to the peak of divinity do not diminish but accentuate their self-possession.[1] They preserve and therefore deepen their private centres. Not only does something of us survive but we survive as ourselves in unity. Constitutionally, after all, the personalization of the universe can only operate by preserving for ever in one supreme person the separate sum of 'persons' born successively in the course of its evolution. God can only be defined as a *centre of centres*. In this complexity lies the perfection of His unity[2] —the only final goal logically attributable to the developments of spirit-matter.

Complexity of God, we have just said. Let us not be frightened by this deduction. The expression is right, but on condition that we correct it in a way that profoundly modifies its value. A complex being, in our present experience, signifies a state which implies for the 'compound' being mutual exclusiveness and eventual disaggregation of its parts. But these two weaknesses (inner opposition and fragility) which we are in danger of regarding as essential to any compound being, can only be effects transitorily connected with the earlier phases of the synthesis. Pushed to its limits, union (being, as we have seen, irreversible) can no longer know either inner obscurities or 'corruption'.

In the first place, no more obscurities or mutual strangeness between the parts. At present it seems inconceivable that persons should enter into contact through the depths of themselves. But this is because they have not yet reached the 'space' in which such a turning about is possible. We must imagine for ourselves thinking molecules interiorized on one another when they reach their

[1] The English word is used.

[2] The more God *is*, the more power He has to centre and perfectly personalize. Consequently unchangingness belongs no less to the richness of an infinite complexity supremely unified than to an essential simplicity. (*Ed.*)

perfect conjunction. A perfect mutual transparency in a perfect self-possession, this is the only pantheistic[1] fusion logically conceivable for souls in the divine milieu.

Consequently there is no possible turning back. Since they have become interior to one another in the interiority of the supreme centre that envelops them, the monads are no longer open to disaggregation. Whether in their separate individuality or in their harmonized collectivity, they have passed the threshold beyond which they can no longer be threatened by any risk of returning to dust. They are once and for all consolidated. Thus the stubborn refusal of our being to construct within it anything but immortality is justified in the result. And so incorruptibility (but this time freed of its connexion with a 'simplicity' hard to understand) which ancient philosophy rightly saw as the most characteristic attribute of spirituality finds its place again in thought.

And now one final point of the first importance remains to be settled before the position and nature of the end can be definitely fixed—the end which it is our whole life's purpose to reach. Since by definition we are 'reality', and multiply our race in reality, the apex of the world clearly cannot be conceived as simply a 'virtual' point of convergence. It must be *real* also. But to what extent is it already *realized*? The one does not seem to follow immediately from the other. Could we not conceive of a universe inclined forward and supported by the birth of a still potential unity in the

[1]Because from the Christian viewpoint the universe is only definitely unified by means of *personal* relations, that is to say under the influence of love, the unification of beings in God cannot be conceived except as operating by fusion (God being born by fusion of the elements of the world or, on the contrary, absorbing them in Him), but in a 'differentiating' synthesis (the elements of the world becoming more themselves the more they converge in God). For the special effect of love is to plunge the beings it draws together more deeply into themselves. In the totalized Christian universe (the 'Pleroma', as St. Paul calls it), God does not ultimately remain alone: He is all in all (*'en pasi panta Theos'*). See *Introduction à la vie chrétienne* (1944), 'Conclusion: Christianisme et panthéisme'.

future? Like Israel awaiting the Messiah? From the structure of a universe of interlocking personalities can we deduce not only the final appearance but the presence today of the divine terminal centre?

In the extra-temporal metaphysics of being this question may seem lacking in respect. Before all creation, proclaim the scholastics, the absolute existed in its fullness. For us who are simply trying to construct a sort of ultra-physics, by combining the sum of our experiments in the most harmonious way, the answer to the problem is not so positive. From the empirical point of view there is no pure act but only a final term to which the serial bundle that envelops us is converging. What kind of actuality must we recognize in this term in order that it may be real?

I should not be surprised if a more profound analysis of the conditions imposed on the world by the laws of union were to lead us one day to recognize in the God of evolution an exact equivalent of the attributes accorded to the '*Ens a se*' by mediaeval philosophy. But if I have not yet reached this point in my thought[1], there are at least two things which I consider gained and which seemed to me sufficient provisionally to guide our march forward.

The first is that though the future centre of the cosmos still presents itself to us with the characteristics of a 'limit', it must be considered as having *from the beginning*, by something in itself, emerged into the absolute. Since everything is supported only by the centre, while the centre rests only upon itself, it must find in itself its own principle of consistence. In this sense, not only does it, as we have already said, constitute a special term at the head of all the series, but it is also in some way out-of-series. In it everything climbs as to a focus of immanence. But everything also descends from it as from a peak of transcendence.

And there is something also I see: that in order to be capable of acting on the wave of personality which its influence raises, it must already have, at every moment, a personality superior to

[1]Since he confines himself here to the realm of ultra-physics. (*Ed.*)

the one it evokes. Within the sphere of thought which arose in the cosmos as a sequel to hominization, the connexions must remain as strict as in the lower spheres of 'matter'. Now within matter, if the energies are to be self-controlled they must fulfil certain precise conditions of homogeneity and potentiality: a molecule only obeys a greater force in its own order of magnitude. This is how we must imagine exchanges of energy within the noosphere. The personal elements in the universe would return to disorder (that is to say to nothingness) if they did not meet some super-personality already actualized, to dominate them. Therefore to balance our activity, there must be in the world around us not only the expectation but the already recognizable face of a universal personality.

Nothing less is needed, as we shall see, to preserve the powers collected in the heart of the individual, of societies and of the world itself from going badly astray.

V THE ENERGY OF PERSONALIZATION

In the course of the preceding sections we have tried to construct logically for the intellect a world on the basis of personality. Let us now enquire what effect this picture would have on the conduct of our lives. What would be the scale of values in a personal universe from the point of view of action?

One first effect of the standpoint here adopted is to reveal in every form of human effort a cosmic value (or stuff) which was not to be seen in any other system. Since the fundamental energy at play in the universe is nothing but a flux of personalization, the bulk of so-called 'moral' relations by which thinking molecules react on one another no longer forms an artificial or secondary domain in nature. Freedom is nothing but the advanced and distinct expression of something that is concealed or dissociated in the physical determinisms. From man onwards, the cosmos is constructed of moral magnitudes. Consequently spiritual action, so despised by science, is now effortlessly placed at the head of the material energies, so far the only ones considered by physicists. We have already been confronted with complex magnitudes like spirit-matter and the personal-universal. We are now led correlatively to fuse into a common dimension two apparently opposite characteristics of experience. We are no longer surrounded by a physical realm and a moral realm. There is only the *physico-moral*.

Let us advance one step further. What name should we give, always in relation to our system, to this physico-moral energy of personalization to which all activities displayed by the stuff of the universe are finally reduced? Only one name is possible, if we are to credit it with the generality and power that it should assume on rising to the cosmic order: *love*.

The physical structure of the universe is love.[1] Let us follow in ourselves, in order to recognize and direct them, the manifestations of this fundamental power of which our life is woven. It seems to me to reveal itself to our consciousness in three successive stages: in woman (for man), in society, in the All—by the sense of sex, of humanity and of the cosmos.

a Sexuality. The mutual attraction of the sexes is so fundamental that any explanation of the world (biological, philosophical or religious) that does not succeed in finding it a *structurally essential* place in its system is virtually condemned. To find such a place for sexuality in a cosmic system based on union is particularly easy. But this place must be clearly defined, both for the future

[1] On 15 August, 1936, that is to say three months after finishing this essay, the author wrote to a friend: 'It gives me great strength, in any case, to recognize that all evolutionary effort can be explained as the justification and development of a love (of God). It is what my mother told me long ago, but it will have taken me a lifetime to integrate this truth into an organic vision of things. It is this effort of integration, I think, that the world must make in order to be converted: as a whole, our world denies personality and God because it believes in the All! Everything depends on convincing it that, on the contrary, it *must* believe in the personal because it believes in the All.'

and the past. What exactly are the essence and direction of 'passionate love' in a universe whose stuff is personality?

In its initial forms, and up to a very high stage in life, sexuality seems identified with propagation. Beings come together to prolong not themselves but what they have gained. So close is the link between coupling and reproduction that philosophers like Bergson have seen in it a proof that life has more existence than living beings; and religions as advanced as Christianity have hitherto based almost the whole of their moral code on the child.

But things look very different from the point of view to which the analysis of a structurally convergent cosmos has brought us. That the dominant function of sexuality was at first to assure the preservation of the species is indisputable. This was so until the *state* of personality was established in man. But from the critical moment of hominization, another more essential role was developed for love, a role of which we are seemingly only just beginning to feel the importance; I mean the necessary synthesis of the two principles, male and female, in the building of the human personality. No moralist or psychologist has ever doubted that these partners find a mutual completion in the play of their reproductive function. But hitherto this has been regarded only as a *secondary* effect, linked as an accessory to the principal phenomenon of reproduction. In obedience to the laws of the personal universe, the importance of these factors is tending, if I am not mistaken, to be reversed. Man and woman for the child, still and for so long as life on earth has not reached maturity. But man and woman for one another increasingly and for ever.

In order to establish the truth of this picture, I cannot do otherwise or better than resort to the sole criterion that has guided our progress throughout this study: that is to say bring the theory into the most perfect possible coherence with a vaster realm of reality. If man and woman were, I will say, principally for the child, then the role and power of love would diminish as human individuality is achieved, and the density of population on the earth is reaching saturation point. But if man and woman are principally for one another, then we imagine that with the growth of humanization they will feel an increasing need to draw closer. Now our experience proves that this is the actual state of things and that the other is not. It must therefore be explained.

In the hypothesis here accepted of a universe in process of personalization, the fact that love is increasing instead of diminishing in the course of hominization has a very natural explanation and extension into the future. In the human individual, as we have already said, evolution does not close on itself, but continues further towards a more perfect concentration, linked with further differentiation, also obtained by union. Woman is for man, we should say, precisely the end that is capable of releasing this forward movement. Through woman and woman alone, man can escape from the isolation in which, even if perfected, he would still be in danger of being enclosed. Hence it is no longer strictly correct to say that the mesh of the universe is, in our experience, the thinking monad. The complete human molecule is already around us: a more synthesized element, and more spiritualized from the start, than the individual personality. It is a duality, comprising masculine and feminine together.

Here the cosmic role of sexuality appears in its full breadth. And here at the same time, the rules appear which will guide us in the mastery of that terrifying energy, in which the power that causes the universe to converge on itself passes through us.

The first of these rules is that love, in conformity with the general laws of creative union, contributes to the spiritual differentiations of the two beings which it brings together. The one must not absorb the other nor, still less, should the two lose themselves in the enjoyments of physical possession, which would signify a lapse into plurality and return to nothingness. This is current experience, but can only be properly understood in the context of spirit-matter. Love is an adventure and a conquest. It survives and develops like the universe itself only by perpetual discovery. The only right love is that between couples whose passion leads them both, one through the other, to a higher possession of their being. The gravity of offences against love therefore is not that they outrage some sort of modesty or virtue. It is that they fritter away, by neglect or lust, the universe's reserves of personalization. This wastage is the true explanation of the disorders of 'impurity'. And at a higher degree in the development of union this same wastage occurs in a subtler form, changing love into a joint egoism.

We have already noted, in our chapter on 'extensions of the personality', the critical phase which being undergoes at the moment when thought is condensed in it. The constituents become reflective and may justifiably feel that they are putting the full stop to evolution; that, under the influence of solitary egoisms, the universe is threatened with disintegration into a dust of separate freedom-particles. The same danger of disintegration appears with doubled intensity at the moment when the couple is newly formed. When two beings between whom a great love is possible manage to meet among a swarm of other beings, they tend immediately to enclose themselves in the jealous possession of their mutual gain. Impelled by the fulfilment that has engulfed them, they try instinctively to shut themselves into one another, to the exclusion of the rest. And even if they succeed in overcoming the voluptuous temptations of absorption and repose, they attempt to reserve the promises of the future for their mutual discovery, as if they constituted a *two-person universe*.

Now after all that we have said about the probable structure of the spirit, it is clear that this dream is only a dangerous illusion. In virtue of the same principle that compelled 'simple' personal elements to complete themselves in the pair, the pair in its turn must pursue the achievements that its growth requires beyond itself. And in two ways. On the one hand it must look outside itself for groupings of the same order with which to associate with a view to centring itself further and this point will be discussed later under the heading, 'The Sense of Humanity'. On the other hand, the centre towards which the two lovers converge by uniting must manifest its personality at the very heart of the circle in which their union wishes to isolate itself. Without coming out of itself, the pair will find its equilibrium only in a third being ahead of it. What name must we give to this mysterious 'intruder'?

For so long as the sexualized elements of the world had not reached the stage of personality, progeny alone could represent the reality in which the authors of generation in some way prolonged themselves. But as soon as love came into play, no longer only between parents but between two persons, the final goal necessarily appeared more or less indistinctly ahead of the lovers, the place at which not only their race but their personality would be at once preserved and completed. Then the 'fall forwards', of which we have already followed the adventures, begins once more. Stage by stage it must go on till the end of the world. And finally it is the total centre itself, much more than the child, that appears necessary for the consolidation of love. Love is a three term function: man, woman and God. Its whole perfection and success are bound up with the harmonious balance of these three elements.

Here we see a great difference between the results we have obtained by our analysis of a personal universe and the rules accepted by old moral systems. For them, purity was generally synonymous with separation of the sexes. Loving implied leaving. One term excluded the other. The 'binomial' man-woman was replaced by the binomial man-God (or woman-God). This was the law of highest virtue. The formula which respects the association of the three terms confronting each other seems to us much more general and satisfactory. Purity, in our opinion, simply denotes the more or less distinct manner in which the ultimate centre of their coincidence appears above the two beings in love. No question here of leaving one another, but only of joining in a greater than themselves. The world does not become divine by suppression but by sublimation. Its sanctity is not an elimination but a concentration of the sap of the earth. Thus the idea of spirit-matter is translated into a new ascesis—laborious, as we shall see, but much more comprehensive and effective than the old.

Sublimation. Therefore conservation. But also, and even more, transformation. If it is true therefore that man and woman will be more united to God the more closely they love one another, it is no less certain that the more they belong to God the more and the more beautifully they will find themselves led to loving one another. In what direction can we imagine this further development of love to take place?

No doubt towards a gradual diminution of the part still (and necessarily) played in sexuality by the marvellous but transitory task of reproduction. Life, as we have established, does not propagate itself for the sake of propagation, but only in order to accumulate the elements necessary for its personalization. When the maturing of its personality is approaching for the earth, men will have to realize that it is for them not simply a question of controlling births, but of increasing to the uttermost the quantity of love liberated from the duty of reproduction. Enforced by this new need, the essentially personalizing function of love will detach itself more or less completely from 'the flesh' which has been for a time the organ of propagation. Without ceasing to be physical, in order to remain physical, love will make itself more spiritual.

Sexuality for the man will be satisfied by pure womanliness. Is this not the dream of chastity translated into reality?[1]

[1]In an essay entitled *L'Évolution de la Chasteté* (1934), Teilhard sketches a more perfect state; the same at which he arrived in *Le Milieu Divin*: '(between) man and woman, designed to carry the spiritualization of the earth to the highest stage, no immediate contact, but convergence at a higher level . . .

'Virginity rests on chastity as thought on life: through a turning about or a single point . . .

'Love is in process of "changing state" within the noosphere. And it is in this new direction that the collective passing of humanity into God is being prepared. This transformation of love is theoretically possible. All that it needs for its realization is that the appeal of the divine personal centre be strongly enough felt to conquer the attraction of nature.'

b The Sense of Humanity. By the love of man and woman a thread is wound that stretches to the heart of the world. But there it is only an infinitesimal element in the bundle gradually collected by the effort of human personalization. The pair only subsists when supported by a centre of conjunction lying ahead of itself. But in addition it only holds together when framed by the collection of couples of the same order surrounding it. The personalizing energy displayed by passionate love must therefore be completed by another form of attraction which will draw the totality of human molecules together. It is this particular form of cohesion, spread throughout the whole noosphere, that we call here 'the sense of humanity'.

First of all, nothing resembling this attraction seems to exist in nature. In place of the mutual sympathy which this theory leads us to foresee, there is, as we have already noted, a mutual repulsion dominant within the human mass. Except in some exceptional cases the 'other' usually appears to be the worst danger that our personality meets in the whole course of its development. The other is a nuisance. The other must be got out of the way.

To explain this disturbing reaction of man to men, it is proper to observe that it does not occur at the level where one can expect to see the emergence of the sense of humanity. In the case of passionate love the attraction is produced directly from individual to individual, depending on nothing more than a chance meeting. In the case of collective links, on the other hand, the attraction can only take place between an individual and an already partially organized collectivity; and this is already more complicated. The man in the street gets in my way because I collide with him as a possible rival. I shall like him as soon as I see him as a partner in the struggle. In contrast to the sexual sense the sense of humanity does not directly touch the persons as such but is something that surrounds them. It is simply because we do not sufficiently perceive this something that we have the impression of disliking one another.

Having made this reservation, we have only to look and we shall recognize by a number of signs all round us the existence and progress of the inter-human cohesion we are seeking.

In the simplest case, that of friendship, 'individuality' is strongly sensed in all its concrete and immediate charm. But another element is already recognizable which brings strength and deep joy to the relationship: a common interest. Great friendships are formed in the pursuit of an ideal, in defence of a cause, in the ups-and-downs of research. Their development is not so much a permeation 'of one by the other' as a joint progress through a new world. In this respect friendship seems to me completely different from spiritual love, with which it is habitually confused. Passionate love, even when spiritual, is by nature exclusive, or at least very limited in the persons it brings together: it is founded on duality. Friendship remains constitutionally open to a growing multiplicity.

In this way the various increasingly extensive groupings in which men are caught up arise often from artificial and forced links which engender no soul, but sometimes also from deep common reactions which bring men together in an extraordinary intimacy.

And so, by insensible transitions, the vast collective unities which will perhaps appear to our descendants as the most characteristic biological phenomenon of our epoch take their birth before our eyes. Communism, Fascism, Nazism etc. . . . all the major currents into which the multiplicity of sporting, educational and social groups eventually coalesce are often condemned as a return to primitive gregariousness. Mistakenly. Life has never known, and has hitherto been incapable of knowing, anything comparable to these mass movements which require for their production a homogeneous layer of consciousness and an extreme rapidity of communication. Long ago the Huns and the Mongols invaded Europe like a cataclysm. This was no more than a directed flood or avalanche. Today, for the first time in the history of the world, the possibility of *reflective masses* has made its appearance. The phenomenon of man has already left the scale of the individual to propagate in a vaster field. It is not therefore repulsion but the mutual attraction of elements that dominates the evolution of the noosphere. And no force of cohesion known to the physical sciences can possibly be as powerful as that. But does this attraction lead, as I claimed, towards a personalization?

Here once more first appearances show themselves unfavourable to the theory. If there is one universal complaint in the world today, it is that of the human personality stifled by the collective monsters which a pitiless necessity of life has compelled us to set up everywhere around us. Great cities, great industries, great economic organizations . . . Heartless and faceless Molochs. Who has not looked back nostalgically some time in his life towards the 'golden age', the family fields, the village workshop or even the forest? Can we really speak of the birth of a soul of humanity? Are we not on the contrary approaching a mechanization of the earth?

I feel as much as anyone the seriousness of the present moment for humanity, and I feel as unwilling as anyone to predict the future. And yet an instinct developed by contact with life's great past tells me that safety for us lies in the same direction as the danger that so dismays us. If in truth (as it certainly seems) the social unification of the earth is the state towards which evolution is drawing us, this transformation cannot contradict the results most clearly achieved by this same evolution in the course of the ages—that is to say the increase of consciousness and individual freedom. Like any other union the collectivization of the earth, rightly conducted, should 'super-animate' us in a common soul. Surely we can already feel the precursory breath of the great wind which is arising, striking us in rapid gusts. In what age of the world has a being experienced more palpable moments of exaltation than man today? Like travellers caught by a current, we should like to turn back. An impossible and fatal course. Safety for us lies ahead, beyond the rapids. There is no turning back. But a sure hand on the tiller and a good compass.

By what signs shall we recognize the reefs that we must every moment avoid, and the path we must follow? We must apply to our course, in so far as it is free, the fundamental law of union. In order not to lose our way on our journey into the future we have only to take our bearings constantly in the direction of a greater personalization, individual or collective.

Individual first. It is perfectly clear that the danger of mechanization has never been greater for the spirit than at this moment when it is approaching a new maximum. One cannot climb a mountain without skirting an abyss. But this risk is not a disaster, and we can avoid a fall. It was the 'organic machine' that first released thought in the human body. Why should it not be the industrial machine that will release it a second time in humanity. We cannot possibly avoid suffering from our early contacts with an incompletely organized mass. But everything that would tend systematically to turn us into termites is wrong and under sentence of death.

Collectivity, then, as requisite condition. By virtue of the rules of union, the associated elements only personalize in themselves under the influence of a more finished dominant personality. It would be no good our trying to avoid the termite colony if the new links being constructed in the world did not derive from a centre recognizable both by our intelligence and our sensibility. The sense of humanity must be of the order of love. Otherwise it will not be human. Society will inevitably become a machine if its successive growths do not step by step culminate in *Someone*. If humanity is not to be oppressive, it must assume a superhuman shape.

And here we are inevitably brought back again to a centre of universal consciousness shining at the apex of evolution. This is the centre which has just torn through the blanket of egoism in which our couple tended jealously to wrap themselves. Now it will save the intricate mass of the noosphere from slavery. And, as we have still to see, by directing our most universal aspirations it will also give the cosmic sense its true significance and full value.

c The Cosmic Sense. I give the name of cosmic sense to the more or less confused affinity that binds us psychologically to the All which envelops us. The existence of this feeling is indubitable, and apparently as old as the beginning of thought. In order that the sense of humanity might emerge, it was necessary for civilization to begin to encircle the earth. The cosmic sense must have been born as soon as man found himself facing the forest, the sea and the stars. And since then we find evidence of it in all our experience of the great and unbounded: in art, in poetry, in religion. Through it we react to the world 'as a whole'[1] as with our eyes to light.

Psychology however is still far from having found a definite place for this profound attraction. Either its specific quality is unrecognized, as if it were perhaps a stray or embryonic form of some other spiritual energy. Or, its value is not accepted, as if it were a residual, almost animal feeling fated to disappear with the complete awakening of reason. Or else, among those who appreciate and foster it, its promptings are interpreted in a dangerous sense as an invitation to anonymous dissolution in the cosmic ocean.

One of the best confirmations, I believe, of the views proposed in these pages is that they easily give a profitable explanation of this polymorphous and powerful feeling. In a personal universe, the cosmic sense immediately finds a natural place; it represents the more or less obscure consciousness in each one of us of the reflective unity in which he is added to all the rest. And thus understood, it shows itself to possess a series of perfectly definite characteristics.

In the first place it appears as a physico-moral magnitude whose nature is to grow. If the universe were breaking up, the cosmic sense might well be in decline: a nostalgia in our souls for the common bough from which the wind of individualization is scattering us like leaves. But if reality, far from dispersing us, is drawing us into convergence with it, then this same feeling must,

[1]The English words used.

by the very structure of the world, inevitably assume a greater clarity and intensity with each step in the progress of humanity. Till now we have perceived it as a deep resonance in our other emotions. But the moment is doubtless coming when, with the rising of the universal centre over the horizon of our consciousness, it will reveal itself as a definite and fundamental element of human psychology.

In a pluralist universe the cosmic sense might be interpreted as an invitation to slackness and diffusion. It has been understood in this sense by so many of the artistic and religious pantheisms till now, for whom admission to the great All signified a dissolvent communion with nature. In the world of the universal-personal the laws of union with the All take precisely the opposite form. It is no longer a question for the element of dispersing over a vast expanse, but on the contrary of centring itself, in harmony with all other centres, on an ultimate centre of all centres. To centre, that is to say to personalize, on an ultimate centre, that is to say on a supreme personality. The only way we have of responding to the obscure promptings of the cosmic sense in us is to push to its final limits a laborious interpretation of the world and of ourselves. Union by differentiation, and differentiation by union. This structural law that we recognized above in the stuff of the universe reappears here as the law of moral perfection, and the sole definition of true pantheism.[1]

The immediate corollary of this discovery is that it is possible for us to ascribe to a precise category this nameless feeling that draws us so powerfully towards nature. Not metaphorically, but in the truest sense of the term, the cosmic sense is a kind of love, and can be nothing else. It is love, because it bears us towards a complementary and unique object of a personal nature. And it must be love because its role is to dominate by consummation the love of man for woman and the love of the human being for all other human beings. In the cosmos as I describe it here, it becomes possible, strange though the expression appears, to *love the uni-*

[1]See note, p. 69.

verse. It is indeed in this act alone that love can develop in bound-less light and power.

We rightly distrust an affection that is too generalized. 'He who loves all loves none', it is habitually said. This danger vanishes, at least in theory, once the All is understood to be personalized: that is to say a definite central figure appearing at the end of a sequence of elementary figures which acquire increasing defini-tion. Directed towards such an object, the heart is in no risk of drying up in impersonal and diffuse aspirations. Without losing contact with the concrete reality of the beings around it, it dis-covers the means of embracing them all together in a feeling which, despite its unlimited extension, preserves the warmth of human affection. One single thing is loved in the end, the loving centre of all convergence. But we can only reach it by completely attaching ourselves to the reality and to the understanding of the particular beings in whose depths it shines.

Hence this unique privilege of the cosmic sense expressed in love. Not only is it a bottomless ocean into which we can plunge indefinitely. But in its 'universalized' dimensions the boundaries vanish between what we call, on the individual scale, the 'I', the rest, the others and, in the 'I' between thought, feelings and action. All these categories, without losing their precise nature, tend to melt into a single motion of apprehension and compre-hension, of 'passion' and action. At this level, multiplicity begins to vanish in the psychic domain. And henceforth a state arises around us in which nothing is to be seen but the collective singularity of a unique action-feeling: the cosmic act of universal personalization.

VI THE PAINS OF PERSONALIZATION

If everything in us and around us is indeed moving towards a great union by love, the world should seemingly be bathed in joy. How is it that on the contrary it is falling more deeply into grief? Why all these tears and blood? How can suffering enter into a personal universe?

My answer to this question, the most anguishing of all for the human mind, will be this: in the universe that I have discussed the problem of evil presents no special difficulty. In fact it finds the most satisfying theoretical solution, and even some indication of a practical one.

A world on the way to concentration of consciousness, you think, would be all joy? On the contrary, I answer. It is just such a world that is the most natural and necessary seat of suffering. Nothing is more beatific than union attained; nothing more laborious than the pursuit of union. For three reasons at least a personalizing evolution is necessarily painful: it is basically a plurality; it advances by differentiation; it leads to metamorphoses.

a The Pain of Plurality. Plurality (a residue of plurality inseparable from all unification in progress) is the most obvious source of our pain. Externally it exposes us to jars and makes us sensitive to these jars. And internally it makes us fragile and subject to countless kinds of physical disorders. Everything that has not 'finished organizing' must inevitably suffer from its residual lack of organization and its possible disorganizations. Such is the state of man.

There is no need to insist on the rigours which this law of plurality inflicts on the corporeal world. But it is to the point of our argument to observe how patently it extends into the physicomoral domain of the personalized universe. Let us look around us. Among the multitude of living beings whose paths cross, there is initially a number of souls made in order to join[1], souls who would have brought one another exactly the beatifying complement that they lack, but who will never recognize one another.

[1]See Baudelaire, *To a woman passing*:

> I do not know where you are hurrying, you do not know
> where I am going,
> Woman I might have loved, woman who knew this was so.

(*Ed.*)

The meetings that bring happiness to our lives depend on the most shocking chances. In the rare cases when an encounter actually takes place, there is the incredible difficulty to be surmounted of maintaining external life contacts. Too often those who love one another best are separated shortly after meeting by the same hazards that brought them together. Even in those exceptional cases where they remain peacefully together, there are great difficulties and dangers in the progress of their inner contact; mazes in which they hear but cannot find one another, blind alleys in which they collide, dividing paths. There are souls who lose their way in one another. And if at last, by supreme success, one comes to the heart of the other, there always remains that final barrier of two minds which, however close they come, never become entirely transparent to one another, because they are not yet, because they cannot be before the final consummation, interiorized in one another. Unions missed, broken unions, incomplete unions. How many disasters, ups and downs or, to put the best complexion on it, how many misunderstandings and estrangements take place even in the most successful unions!

b The Pain of Differentiation. As if it were not enough for us to have to suffer the disorders and exteriority resulting from the residual plurality of the world, we meet a second cause of suffering in the very efforts we must make to escape from this state of multiplicity. Here there appears an underlying condition of evolution, by which the laws of physical chemistry and those of physical morality join in a way still confusing to our minds: unification is a labour. In a very true sense, as we were just saying, plurality's only support is the unity ahead. And yet this return to equilibrium is a laborious ascent, which only takes place by overcoming a true ontological inertia. Life has therefore, even in its very highest forms, a continual inclination to stop or even fall back. *Duration is a climb.*

In the excitement of the chase and the joy of conquest, we hardly notice this fundamental characteristic of the process. We forget the pain in order to think only of the joy of growing. And yet this pain is never absent. In order to unify in ourselves or unite with others, we must change, renounce, give ourselves; and this violence to ourselves partakes of pain. In common language, the most candid vehicle of human experience, the idea of perfection is unfailingly expressed in metaphors of toil and ascent. Every advance in personalization must be paid for: so much union, so much suffering. This rule of equivalence governs all transformations of spirit-matter. And nothing can permit of escape from it.

c The Pain of Metamorphosis. If the pain of differentiation which is inherent in union generally affects us little, it is because we palpably associate with it the consciousness of our progress. The anguish of feeling ourselves apparently threatened in the most secret corners of our own hearts is very much more bitter. It can truly be said that real pain entered the world with man, when for the first time a reflective consciousness became capable of observing its own diminution. The only true *evil* is suffered by personality. In what form does death present itself in the personal universe that we have outlined here?

I will answer, as a metamorphosis.

We must return again to this important point on which we have already touched when considering the formation and consummation of the personality: no physical agent can grow indefinitely without reaching the phase of a change of state. For a more or less long period, things simply vary, without ceasing to remain recognizably themselves. And then at a given moment a complete reconstitution of the elements becomes necessary, so that it may be of a magnitude to enter a new realm of possible progress. The force of personalization, in which we believed we had recognized the mainspring of evolution, apparently meets with these discontinuities in the course of its development. On reaching a certain limit of concentration, the personal elements find themselves faced with a threshold to be crossed before they can enter the sphere of action of a centre of higher order. It is not only necessary for them at that moment to rouse themselves from the inertia which tends to immobilize them. The moment has come also for them to surrender to a transformation which appears to take from them all that they have already acquired. *They can grow no greater without changing.* Then comes the agony of losing ourselves in the monstrous mass of humanity that awaits us or the still greater agony of escaping by the swift or slow dissolution of the body from the totality of the framework of experience into which we were born.

Deaths, death, are no more than critical points scattered on the road of union. In this simple solution do we not get a complete measure of the explicatory value of the hypothesis we have assumed? Not only does the problem of evil in its most acute form find its natural answer, linked with an *optimistic interpretation* of the universe, in the perspective of a personal universe. But this theoretical interpretation also lets us glimpse a remedy for the pain of the world and a way out from it.

d The Shrinking of Evil. The evil in evil does not lie in the pain, but in the feeling of diminishing through pain. The greatest suffering you can think of will disappear, or even dissolve in a kind of pleasure, provided you can discover a correlatively proportionate achievement of which it has been the price. Hunger, thirst and wounds are unbearable in passivity and inaction. They no longer count, or even do not exist, in the fever of an attack or a discovery. Let us think what will be sufficient, even in our present unorganized state, to compensate humanity for the anguish of its ills? Simply for consciousness to awake to an object born from its sufferings. The idea of a personalization of the universe will bring that faith and that hope.

I know that the world is vast and its perfection can be glimpsed only through such changes that comfort discovered at such a distance may seem absurd. But we allow so many treasures to escape through timidity or laziness, simply because we think we have found a good reason for not trying. Instead of standing on the shore and proving to ourselves that the ocean cannot carry us, let us venture on its waters—just to see. It seems to us impossible that a human life could find joy by losing itself consciously in the universal being. Let us risk taking this action. Let us seek our essential satisfaction in the thought that we are serving and preserving a personal universe by our endeavours. If a natural centre of things really exists, as these pages have attempted to show, this centre will react. We shall not see it any more distinctly than the age of the world allows. But because we shall have turned towards that centre, its reality will make itself felt by the light and heat which will descend into us.

From this progressive illumination as much as from a better organization of material life and society we can hope for a gradual diminution of evil on the earth. While they have still not dissolved in a higher atmosphere, the dark clouds around us may yet be transfigured. Pain is virtually conquered by the cosmic sense. Despite so many contrary appearances, the world might here and now arise in joy, as the theory of union foretells, if it understood the mystery of personality developing within it.

VII CONCLUSION: THE RELIGION OF PERSONALITY

An attempted solution of the problem of evil was the final test of value to which we could submit the hypothesis developed in this essay. I think I can now conclude that the hypothesis succeeds, and that it generally satisfies the condition that we demanded of a world picture at the beginning: that it shall render the universe totally coherent with itself.

I do not think there is any better or even any other natural centre of total coherence of things than the human personality. Starting from this complex mesh in which the soul is bound by the flesh, the cosmos winds away backwards and weaves itself forward according to a simple law satisfactory at once to the mind and for action. The false contradictions between spirit and matter, universality and personality, moral forces and physical powers vanish. Under pressure of the stress of personalization, the elements advance in an infallible direction, though by way of those gropings and chances that our science records. They suffer and die, but these metamorphoses do not deprive them of what they would have no reason or appetite for acquiring if their 'I' had been taken from them. In the convergent movement that makes all things into a whole, unity ceases to oppose multiplicity, and a monism takes shape which respects both the poverty and richness of experience of plurality.

Now to justify a perspective of such natural harmony, we have had recourse to no philosophy. Neither explicitly nor implicitly has the notion of an absolute best, or of causation, or of finality occurred in our argument. An experimental law of recurrence of experience and a rule of succession in time are all that we present to the positivist wisdom of our century.

No metaphysics, let me repeat, but an ultra-physics. And yet, as I have still to say, a mysticism and a religion also.

We have not so far written that word. But those who have followed my argument will certainly have used it many pages back. Like every other form of adherence to a cosmic hope, the doctrine of the personal universe has exactly those characteristics of universality and faith which are, in the broad sense of the term, distinctive of religion. But the religion it introduces has in addition two associated characteristics which seemed, to their mutual detriment, destined to be perpetual opposites in religious systems: personalism and pantheism.

Is such a position *practically* possible?

I say, yes. And the proof is that it is already virtually realized and lived in Christianity.

Believe it or not, the ideas contained in the present essay, although obviously influenced by the Gospels, were not born into my mind from the specifically Christian part of myself. On the contrary, they arose in antagonism to it; and they are so completely independent of it that I should find myself singularly troubled in my faith if something in them were to contradict Christian doctrine. But in fact (at the cost, I admit, of some struggles) the contrary has hitherto always been the case. Far from contradicting my profound tendencies towards pantheism, Christianity, rightly understood, has unceasingly, *precisely because it is the saviour of personality*, guided, clarified and also confirmed them by supplying a precise object and a starting point for experimental verification.

Let me explain myself.

Christianity is essentially the religion of personality. And it is so to such a degree that it is at present in danger of losing its influence on the human soul by the kind of inability it shows of understanding the organic links of which the universe is composed. For ninety per cent of those who view Him from outside, the Christian God looks like a great landowner administering his estates, the world. Now this conventional picture, which is too well justified by appearances, corresponds in no way to the dogmatic basis or point of view of the Gospels. And for this reason. The essence of Christianity is neither more nor less than a belief in the unification of the world in God by the Incarnation. All the rest is only secondary explanation or illustration. In view of this, so long as human society had not emerged from the 'neolithic', family phase of its development (that is to say until the dawn of the modern scientific-industrial phase) clearly the Incarnation could only find symbols of a juridical nature to express it. But since our modern discovery of the great unities and vast energies of the cosmos, the ancient words begin to assume a new and more satisfying meaning. To be the alpha and omega, Christ must, without losing his precise humanity, become co-extensive with the physical expanse of time and space. In order to reign on earth, He must 'super-animate' the world. In Him henceforth, by the whole logic of Christianity, personality expands (or rather centres itself) till it becomes universal. Is this not exactly the God we are waiting for?

I will not go so far as to say that this religious renaissance is yet self-conscious. In all realms, the old framework resists hardest when it is at breaking-point. But my experience of Christianity allows me to affirm this: whatever formalisms may still persist, the transformation of which I speak has already taken place in the most living parts of the Christian organism. Beneath a surface pessimism, individualism or juridicism, Christ the King is *already worshipped today as the God of progress and evolution.*

Earlier, when I was analysing the conditions that a centre of the universe must satisfy, I spoke of a love stronger than sexual attraction, of a love which would embrace the whole earth, of a love which would find the heart of the universe. It might seem that I was speculating on a utopia. But all I was doing in reality was to develop the potentialities contained in the factual reality of Christianity. In the actual simplicity of his worship, the believer perceives and performs all that I seemed to be dreaming of.

With this coincidence as evidence, I begin to think in the most critical and positivistic parts of my being that the Christian phenomenon might well be what it claims to be, and what every theory of a personal universe appeals to as a final test of its truth: the reflexion of the supreme consciousness on the elements of consciousness it has collected—in fact a revelation.

Unpublished, Peking, 4 May, 1936.

THE PHENOMENON OF SPIRITUALITY

Around us, bodies present various qualities: they are warm, coloured, electrified, heavy. But also in certain cases they are living, conscious. Beside the phenomena of heat, light and the rest studied by physics, there is, just as real and *natural*, the *phenomenon of spirituality*.

The phenomenon of spirit has rightly attracted man's attention more than any other. We are coincidental with it. We feel it from within. It is the very thread of which the other phenomena are woven for us. It is the thing we know best in the world since we are itself, and it is for us everything. And yet we never come to an understanding concerning the nature of this fundamental element.

For some, heirs to almost all the spiritualist philosophies of former times, the spirit is something so special and so high that it could not possibly be confused with the earthly and material forces which it animates. Incomprehensibly associated with them, it impregnates them but does not mix with them. There is a world of souls and a world of bodies. Spirit is a 'meta-phenomenon'.

For others, on the contrary, more or less belated representatives of nineteenth-century thought, spirit seems something so small and frail that it becomes accidental and secondary. In face of the vast material energies to which it adds absolutely nothing that can be weighed or measured, the 'fact of consciousness' can be regarded as negligible. It is an 'epi-phenomenon'.

I propose in these pages to develop a third viewpoint towards which a new physical science and a new philosophy seem to be converging at the present day: that is to say that spirit is neither super-imposed nor accessory to the cosmos, but that it quite simply represents the higher state assumed in and around us by the primal and indefinable thing that we call, for want of a better name, the 'stuff of the universe'. Nothing more; and also nothing less. Spirit is neither a meta- nor an epi-phenomenon; it is *the* phenomenon.

To establish the value of this new viewpoint, which is charged with moral consequences, my only form of argument will be that universally employed by modern science, that and that alone: by which I mean the argument of 'coherence'. In a world whose single business seems to be to organize itself in relation to itself that is by definition the more *true*, which better harmonizes in relation to ourselves a larger body of facts. If therefore I can succeed in showing that, regarded from the point of view I have chosen, the universe harmonizes better with our experience, thoughts and actions than the two contrary viewpoints, I shall have established in so far as is possible the truth of my thesis.

Let us make the attempt.

I SPIRITUALIZATION

If we wish to appreciate the phenomenon of spirit at its true value, we must first of all familiarize ourselves with the idea of its real breadth. At first sight the conscious portion of the world presents itself in the form of discontinuous, tiny and ephemeral fragments: a bright dust of individualities, a flight of shooting stars. In the second chapter of this essay we shall have to return with a keener eye to the meaning and value inherent in each of these sparks. For the moment it suits us to assume the greatest possible distance from their distracting and minimizing singularity. What are the dimensions of the magnitude that we call 'spirit', *if we take it as a whole*? I am going to show that, rightly regarded, they are the dimensions of the universe itself.

a The Spirit's Present. If we wish to discern the phenomenon of spirit in its entirety, we must first educate our eyes to perceiving collective realities. Because we are ourselves individuals, life around us affects us principally on the individual scale. Atoms ourselves, we at first see only other atoms. But it does not require much reflexion to discover that animate bodies are not as separate from one another as they appear. Not only are they all, by the mechanism of reproduction, related by birth. But by the very process of their development, a network of living connexions (psychological, economic, social, etc.) never for a moment ceases to hold them in a single tissue, which becomes more complicated and tenacious the further they evolve. Like drops of water scattered in the sand and subjected to the same pressure, that of the layer to which they belong; like electrical charges distributed along a single conductor and subjected to the same potential; so conscious beings are in truth only different local manifestations of a mass which contains them all. To the extent that it is subject to experiment, the phenomenon of spirit is not a divided mass; it displays a general manner of being, a collective state peculiar to our world. In other words, scientifically speaking, there are no *spirits* in nature. But there is *a spirit*, physically defined by a certain tension of consciousness on the surface of the earth. This animated covering of our planet may with advantage be called the biosphere—or more precisely (if we are only considering its thinking fringe) the noosphere.

b The Spirit's Past. Let us now make one more effort to transcend individuality; and, having measured the spatial extension of the phenomenon of spirit in the present, let us try to assess its depth in the past. Here, thanks to the recent efforts of history, the establishment of perspectives is particularly easy. Certain minds may still hesitate before the notion of a biosphere. No one can any longer doubt that in so far as it exists, it is rooted over its whole surface in the abyss of past centuries. Spirituality is not a recent accident, arbitrarily or fortuitously imposed on the edifice of the world around us; it is a deeply rooted phenomenon, the traces of which we can follow with certainty backwards as far as the eye can reach, in the wake of the movement that is drawing us forward. As far back as we can recognize a surface of the earth, that surface is inhabited. It is as if no planet can reach a certain stage in its sidereal evolution without breaking into life. But this is not all. The consciousness that we see filling the avenues of the past does not flow simply like a river which carries an unchanging water past ever changing banks. It transforms itself in the course of its journey; it evolves; life has a movement *of its own*. If we follow it backwards in time, we see it reducing the organic complexity of its forms and the range of its spontaneity. Nervous systems become increasingly rudimentary. And to judge from the present survivors of these ancient stages, the animate world disappears at the farthest end into a swarm of living particles that are hardly separate from molecular energies. Inversely, in the direction of the arrow of time, cellular constructions are formed and, step by step with a growth in complexity, consciousness increases its powers of internal clairvoyance and interconnexion until, at the level of man, reflective thought bursts forth.

c Birth of the Spirit. Hence our evidence that, from a purely scientific and empirical standpoint, the true name for 'spirit' is 'spiritualization'. Taken as a whole, in its temporal and spatial totality, life represents the goal of a *transformation* of great breadth, in the course of which what we call 'matter' (in the most comprehensive sense of the word) turns about, furls in on itself, *interiorizes* the operation covering, so far as we are concerned, the whole history of the earth. The phenomenon of spirit is not therefore a sort of brief flash in the night; it reveals a gradual and systematic passage from the unconscious to the conscious, and from the conscious to the self-conscious. It is a cosmic *change of state*.

This irrefutably explains the links and also the contradictions between spirit and matter. And in a sense they are both fundamentally the same thing[1], as the neo-materialists allege; but between them lies also a point of deflection which makes them in some way the opposite of one another, as the ancient spiritualists maintained. All antinomy between souls and bodies disappears in the hypothesis of a movement that has reached its 'critical point'. And the horizon is then swept clear for new perspectives.

d The Future of the Spirit. Recognition that the phenomenon of spirit is *a change of state* greatly simplifies our views of the universe. But this discovery has another advantage; it lights the forward march of the world around us. The majority of changes of state studied by the physical sciences affect quantities limited and peculiar to matter and submitted to localized energies: melting ice, a substance volatilized. In the case of the inward furling '*sui generis*' from which consciousness is born, the phenomenon takes place under conditions of an entirely different order. On the one hand the primordial element that we have called 'the stuff of the universe' is modified by vitalization in precisely its most universal character: not only in one of its secondary properties (depending on a particular degree of molecular or atomic complexity) but in its most fundamental condition, which is that of being or not being interiorized. In other words matter undergoes animation not as a representative of this or that specialized form of matter, but simply because it is matter; in virtue of its basic unity, it is affected in its entirety by metamorphosis. Moreover, just because this metamorphosis extends by right to the whole imaginable expanse of reality, no external cause seems experimentally assignable for the transformation's occurrence. We are in the presence of a kind of autonomous process and inner spon-

[1]'From a purely scientific and empirical standpoint', as is said in the preceding paragraph. (*Ed.*)

taneity, comparable alone in its universality to the mysterious dissipation of energy recognized in the cosmos by modern physics. At a first approximation, we have been able to note by direct observation that the phenomenon of the spirit is coextensive with the very evolution of the earth. We must now limitlessly enlarge these frontiers which already seem so great. In us, beneath our eyes, not only the earth but the universe is concentrating *itself* in thought, exactly as, symmetrically at the other end, it is disaggregating *itself* into amorphous energy. The phenomenon of spirit is therefore one of the two most fundamental cosmic movements that we can grasp experientially. And since, very probably, these two contrary movements (that is to say vitalization and the dissipation of energy) are merely the opposite poles of a single cosmic event of which the positive or synthesizing term is the most significant, it is finally *the* outstanding cosmic movement, the movement on which everything depends and which nothing explains; it is indeed—and this is our thesis—*the phenomenon*.

Now this quality immediately assures it three properties of which the remainder of this essay will examine the substance: it is irresistible (that is to say infallible); it is irreversible; it is totalizing.

Irresistible, first of all. No human force can prevent a heated bar of iron from expanding. No known action seems capable of arresting the decomposition of a radioactive substance. What power could prevent the mainspring of the world from action? If the world is really bound as a whole for consciousness, nothing could possibly oppose the growth of spirit. No shocks, no violence. But the calm and certain ascent of a high-pressure fluid that overcomes all obstacles, profits by every weak point and filters through all the pores of matter, *infallibly*.

Irreversible, next, as a result of being irresistible. If in fact the pressure of spirit is on the one side irresistible, this is a sign that it must victoriously attain its natural goal. But if on the other this goal reveals itself as the infinite ahead, this is a proof that it must succeed in propagating itself interminably. Now this certainly seems to be the case. For all magnitudes registered by the physical sciences we know or suspect a ceiling which they cannot approach without developing certain antagonisms by which they annihilate themselves; an increasing physical inertia, engendered by their motion itself, may at a given moment interrupt their growth of speed. But nothing of this sort seems to apply in the case of consciousness, except perhaps the imperfection of transitory organisms that are quickly abandoned, like those whose remains are scattered on the roads of history. Theoretically, the phenomenon of spirit develops a magnitude that we think of as indefinitely perfectible, and consequently never self-saturated. *Functionally* it is sustained by its own growth, each degree of consciousness at a given moment existing only as an introduction to a higher consciousness: so that we cannot see how, from a mechanical point of view, its progress could be stopped. *Psychologically*, it is nourished by the very feeling of its boundless future: for a reflective being would automatically cease to act if it glimpsed the simple possibility of an impassable limit to its ascent. All this taken together implies that the phenomenon of spirit imagines and considers itself to be *by right* irreversible. For it is irreversible *in fact*, since its progress is, as we have said, irresistible. And, in fact, *historically*, consciousness on earth has never ceased to expand. This simple observation should suffice to show us that, for the progress of the spirit, the universe is completely *free ahead*.

Totalizing, last of all. And this by very virtue of the idea of change of state. Water passes into the steam that rises from it. So any physical evolution that we can imagine, even the highest, must preserve even while sublimating a certain gift that it has received from below. Quality and quantity are structurally linked in nature. If therefore the phenomenon of spirit, as we have assumed, truly expresses a cosmic transformation, it must, in order to be homogeneous with the rest of our experience, obey a definite law of conservation and transmission. A certain mass of 'raw' (or 'exteriorized') being has been taken up in the course of the universe's spiritualization, and this must be 'interiorized' at the conclusion of the operation if this operation is to be successful (as it *infallibly* must be). So much matter, so much spirit.

Considered in its broadest dimensions and its most distant future, the phenomenon of spirit therefore ultimately represents the certain and definite appearance of a cosmic quantum of consciousness: that is to say in fact (since the two terms are identical) *a quantum of personality.*

And here, by this last word, we are brought back to a consideration of the individual centres, which we momentarily abandoned in order to open up wider perspectives.

II PERSONALIZATION

In order to define the nature of the change of cosmic state of which the phenomenon of spirit consists, we made use of the term 'interiorization'. But we might equally well have said 'concentration', since the inward furling from which consciousness is born could not be established except around a centre of perspective and action.

Therefore if we try to imagine the final condition towards which the spiritual transformation taking place is apparently guiding the world, we find ourselves impelled to express it in the form of a *monocentrism*: the All, becoming self-reflective upon a single consciousness. How is it then that, in precise contradiction to these expectations, the universe appears to us today typically particulate, that is to say 'polycentric'? Whence arises the break-up into fragmentary consciousnesses of a reality which, observed from above, seemed to us so powerfully homogeneous in its totality? Why the myriad instead of the monad we expected? What is the significance in nature of the atom, the molecule, the individual, the personal element?

To explain scientifically is, as we said above, to include the facts in a general coherent interpretation. To interpret the pluralism of the world around us, others have resorted to the idea of initial accidents which broke the primal unity of things. From the strictly 'phenomenal' point of view, which we have assumed in this essay, another hypothesis seems simpler, more probable and more fruitful than this pulverization of secondary origin. Everything that happens in the world, we would say, suggests that the unique centre of consciousness around which the universe is furling could only be formed gradually, by successive approximations, through a series of diminishing concentric spheres, each of which in turn engenders the next; each sphere being moreover formed of elementary centres charged with a consciousness that increases as their radius diminishes. By means of this mechanism, each newly appearing sphere is charged in its turn with the consciousness developed in the preceding spheres, carries it a degree higher in each of the elementary centres that compose it, and transmits it a little further on towards the centre of total convergence. Each element of consciousness in the world is therefore to be defined by the sphere to which it belongs, by its position on this sphere and at the same time by the movement which carries it towards the following sphere. And the final centre of the whole system appears at the end both as the final sphere and as the centre of all the centres spread over this final sphere. Seen in this way, the atomic structure of the world is simply the expression of a law of construction inherent in the phenomenon of spirit; it is essential and existed from the beginning. Let us accept this hypothesis after seeing what it explains in the present, let us ask what it allows us to foresee in the future.

1. The first thing which this hypothesis explains is the distribution and relative position of the various forms of consciousness (or unconsciousness) around us in the world.

Right at the bottom, forming a group apart, there are first of all the multiple so-called 'material' spheres. Matter is habitually regarded as inanimate, and this is the source of all our difficulties in understanding it. We now discover that it may simply correspond (to the extent that it exists) to a state of consciousness so extended and fragmentated that its elements are only visible to us in their statistical properties, that is to say in the form of inflexible, completely 'dis-animated' laws. From this viewpoint, material determinisms cease to provide the skeleton of the world; they are merely a secondary effect in the cosmos arising from the mass of elementary spheres. They are the true 'epi-phenomenon'.

In a higher group of spheres, the particles stand out more or less distinctly from the mass. Individuals emerge from great numbers, and consciousness appears. But for a long time these are still only loose unities in which the soul does not seem to be fixed or to recognize itself except confusedly among the incredible complexity of mechanisms which are the evolutionary condition of life. Such in our experience are plants and animals.

At last, in a final phase, thought appears, so scrupulously prepared over so long a time that nothing quivers when it appears in nature, yet so dense that everything bends and shines by its influence. Because no apparent break in the chain of zoological forms separates us from the other animals, natural scientists have for a long time underestimated the biological importance of man. They have invented a *genus* for him. But in reality man marks nothing less than the origin of a new era in the history of the earth. In him for the first time in the realm open to our experience, the universe has become conscious of itself, *personalized*. There is a greater distance in fact between thought and simple organic life than between organic life and so-called inanimate matter. The phenomenon of spirit has entered into a higher and decisive phase by becoming the phenomenon of man.

2. And now a further problem presents itself; standing on what our hypothesis defines as the last formed of the spheres of consciousness, what can we human beings expect from the further developments of the phenomenon of spirit? Where are we brought as individuals by the change of state that is transforming the world into spirit? What lies ahead, and what will become of us?

Logically, the answer to this question is simple. If the concentration of the universe into a single consciousness really obeys the law of recurrence that we imagine, other spheres must exist in the future and, inevitably, a supreme centre in which all the personal energy represented by human consciousness must be gathered and 'super-personalized'. We are moving towards a higher state of general consciousness, which is linked with a further synthesis of our particular consciousnesses. But here we are confronted with an apparently insuperable difficulty. In man, by virtue of reflexion, a fragment of cosmic consciousness is definitely individualized. But how can we imagine that this portion once shaped can afterwards join other like fragments in the building of a super-consciousness? To become super-conscious, it must unite itself with others, we said. But precisely in order to give itself, must it not decentre, that is to say become less conscious of itself? There seems to be a contradiction in this. In order to advance further, the spirit of the world, having become personalized material, would have to undergo another and further fusion. But precisely because it is composed of persons, it seems to have lost the faculty of totalization. Can it be that by entering the personal stage *in a form that is still plural* consciousness has automatically barred the way towards a higher synthesis, and is condemned to remain indefinitely fragmentated? Can it be that the phenomenon of spirit has been immobilized by its own progress before it could reach the natural goal of its development?

The solution of this paradox is to be found by making a distinction between two entirely opposite sorts of union: union by dissolution and union by differentiation. When we imagine that 'persons' cannot totalize (because their totalization would abolish the personalities that it set out to 'add to one another') we are instinctively thinking of rivers flowing into the sea, of salt dissolving in the ocean, of matter breaking down into cosmic energy. But these are deceptive analogies drawn from cases in which the unitive medium is indefinitely widespread: 'centrifugal' union by common relaxation or dissolution in an imagined homogeneous unconsciousness. In fact, in the case of spirit, by very virtue of the 'centripetal' movement of the spheres of consciousness (as we have accepted it) the phenomenon tends towards an exactly opposite result. In this convergent universe, all the lower centres unite, but by inclusion in a more powerful centre. Therefore they are all preserved and completed by joining together. Union of concentration (the *only* true union) does not destroy but emphasizes the elements it swallows. Reflective human units can therefore undergo this operation without being destroyed or distorted. Despite appearances, persons can still serve as elements in a further synthesis, *because the precise result of their union is to differentiate them.*

Union in the personal differentiates. Three series of important corollaries follow from this proposition; and these will successfully define the actions of the phenomenon of spirit.

a First. As regards our individual destinies we can see a justification ahead for our hope of a personal immortality, which seems to be the *necessary* natural compensation, for thinking beings, of a death that *they have become capable of foreseeing.* On the one hand, the irresistible and infallible spiritualization of the world would not succeed if the conscious particle represented by each one of us were not to pass into an irreversible and totalizing term of transformation; and on the other hand this passage of what is us into what is other, far from threatening our ego, has precisely the effect of consolidating it. Death, in which we seem to disappear, thus reveals itself as representing a simple phase of growth; it marks our accession into a super-human sphere of self-consciousness, of personality.

b Second. As regards the final nature of the spirit into which all spirituality converges, that is to say all the personality in the world, we see that its supreme simplicity contains a prodigious complexity. In that spirit, on the one hand, all the elements into which the personal consciousness of the world appeared in the beginning to be broken up (that is to say at the moment of hominization) are carried to their maximum individual differentiation by maximum union with the All, and then extended without becoming confused with one another. And on the other hand, in this spirit, essentially needed for the unification without confusion of these *unmixable* centres, a distinct and autonomous centre is discovered as necessary, which is itself personal and radiates over the myriad of inferior personalities: the sum of all the past and the ultimate focal point of the future.

c Third. As regards the direction of our present activity, we observe that, to complete ourselves, we must pass into a greater than ourselves. Survival and also 'super-life' await us in the direction of a growing consciousness and love of the universal. All our action should be organized—that is to say our morality should be shaped—towards reaching (and at the same time bringing into being) this pole.

III MORAL APPLICATION

For the 'old-style' spiritualist who regards the spirit as a meta-phenomenon, as for the modern materialist who chooses to see it only as an epi-phenomenon, the world of moral relationships forms a separate department of nature. For different reasons, forces and connexions of a moral kind are for both less physically real than the energies of matter. For us who see the development of consciousness as *the* essential phenomenon of nature, things appear in a very different light. If indeed as we have assumed the world culminates in a thinking reality, the organization of personal human energies represents the supreme stage of cosmic evolution on earth; and morality is consequently nothing less than the higher development of mechanics and biology. The world is ultimately constructed by moral forces; and reciprocally, the function of morality is to construct the world: an entirely new valuation leading to an altered programme of morality.

a Morality of Balance and Morality of Movement. Morality arose largely as an empirical defence of the individual and society. Ever since intelligent beings began to be in contact, and consequently in friction, they have felt the need to guard themselves against each other's encroachments. And once an arrangement was in practice discovered which more or less guaranteed to each one his due, this system itself felt the need to guarantee itself against the changes which would call its accepted solutions into question and disturb the established social order. Morality has till now been principally understood as a fixed system of rights and duties intended to establish a static equilibrium between individuals, and at pains to maintain it by a *limitation* of energies, that is to say of force.

This conception rested in the last resort on the idea that every human being represented a sort of absolute term in the world, whose existence had to be protected from all encroachment from without. It is transformed from top to bottom, if one recognizes, as we have just done, that man on earth is no more than an element destined to complete himself cosmically in a higher consciousness in process of formation. Now the problem confronting morality is no longer how to preserve and protect the individual, but how to guide him so effectively in the direction of his anticipated fulfillments that the 'quantity of personality' still diffuse in humanity may be released in fullness and security. The moralist was up to now a jurist, or a tight-rope walker. He becomes the technician and engineer of the spiritual energies of the world. The highest morality is henceforth that which will best develop the phenomenon of nature to its upper limits. No longer to protect but to develop, by awakening and convergence, the individual riches of the earth.

Let us sketch in a few lines the features of this morality of movement. Three principles axiomatically define the value of human actions:

i. *only* finally good is what makes for the growth of the spirit on earth.

ii. good (at least basically and partially) is *everything* that brings a spiritual growth to the world.

106

iii. finally *best* is what assures their highest development to the spiritual powers of the earth.

These three rules clearly modify or complete, to a substantial extent, the idea we have of goodness and perfection.

In virtue of the first, many things seemed allowed by the morality of balance, which we find to be forbidden by the morality of movement. Provided that he did not steal his neighbour's wife or goods, a man could think himself authorized to use as he thought best or leave dormant that part of life which belonged to him. We now see that no promise or custom is lawful if it does not tend to *the service* of the power within it. Money morality was dominated by the idea of exchange and fairness: so much for so much. The level of a liquid in two communicating vessels. It must henceforth obey the idea of energy in movement: riches only become good to the extent that they *work* for the benefit of the spirit. The morality of love was satisfied by the material founding of a family, love itself being considered a secondary attraction subordinate to procreation. It must now consider as its fundamental object to give that love just the incalculable spiritual power that it is capable of developing between husband and wife. Finally, the morality of the individual was principally ordained to prevent him from doing harm. In future it will forbid him a neutral and 'inoffensive' existence, and compel him strenuously to free his autonomy and personality to the uttermost.

By virtue of the second rule, correlatively many things seemed to be forbidden by the morality of balance which become virtually permitted or even obligatory by the morality of movement. Precisely because it was satisfied with order, so long as that order prevented the mechanism of humanity from grinding and over-heating, the morality of balance did not trouble to find out whether some spiritual possibilities were not excluded from the framework it had constructed. Being unable to find an easy place and justification for them, out of timidity or playing for safety, it allowed a world of energy to be lost in every realm. In a morality of movement, everything that contains an ascending force of consciousness is recognized under that head and within those limits as fundamentally good: all that has to be done is to isolate that goodness by analysis and to disengage it by sublimation.

And thus, *by virtue of the third rule* we discover the new idea of a *moralization*, to be understood as the indefinitely continuous discovery and conquest of the animate powers of the earth. To the morality of balance ('closed morality') the moral world might seem a definitely bounded realm. To the morality of movement ('open morality') the same world appears as a higher sphere of the universe, much richer than the lower spheres of matter in unknown powers and unsuspected combinations. The boldest mariners of tomorrow will sail out to explore and humanize the mysterious ocean of moral energies. To try everything and force everything in the direction of the greatest consciousness[1]; this, in a universe recognized to be in a state of spiritual transformation, is the general and highest law of morality: to limit *force*[2] (unless for the purpose of obtaining even more force) *is sin*.

These perspectives will appear absurd to anyone who does not see that ever since its beginnings life has been a groping, an adventure, a risk. They grow like an irresistible idea, however, on the horizon of new generations. The future belongs to them. But on one condition: that, with a speed equal to their own, a palpable centre of attraction and illumination arises in the sky to light them.

b God's Spiritual Function. A morality of balance can be constructed and subsist closed in on itself. Since it sets out only to adjust associated elements to one another, it is sufficiently determined and sustained by a mutual agreement of the parties it reconciles. A minimum of internal frictions in a regulated state is

[1]Consciousness-love, see below, *Human Energy*. (*Ed.*)

[2]Force here signifies energy and love. See below, *Human Energy*, Section VI, 'Love, a Higher Form of Human Energy', p. 145; 'Not force but love above us . . .', p. 152 (*Ed.*)

both the ideal to which it tends and a sign that it has reached it.

In the morality of movement, on the contrary, which is only defined by relation to a state or object to be reached, it is imperative that the goal shall shine with enough light to be desired and held in view. Examined in its external development, the phenomenon of spirit appeared to us to depend on a common centre of total organization. Observed now in its internal functioning, it brings us—as was inevitable—face to face with this pole of attraction and total determination.

A morality of balance may logically be agnostic and engrossed in possession of the present moment. A morality of movement necessarily inclines towards the future, in pursuit of a God.

In these pages I shall deliberately refrain from again making 'a critique of religions'. But I think it necessary to state two conditions, cohering to the views developed in this essay, which the God we are seeking must satisfy, if He is to be capable of sustaining and directing the phenomenon of spirit.

The first condition is that He shall combine in his singularity the evolutionary extension of all the fibres of the world in movement: a God of cosmic synthesis in whom we can be conscious of advancing and joining together by spiritual transformation of all the powers of matter.

And the second condition is that this same God shall act in the course of this synthesis as a first nucleus of independent consciousness: a supremely personal God, from whom we are the more distinguishable the more we lose ourselves in Him.

These two in no way contradictory conditions immediately result from the characteristics recognized above in the cosmic genesis of the spirit: a universal God to be realized by effort, and yet a personal God to be submitted to in love. If the world is really moving within consciousness, He is the indispensable 'mover' of all further progress of life.

In short, humanity has reached the biological point where it must either lose all belief in the universe or quite resolutely worship it.[1] This is where we must look for the origin of the present crisis in morality. But it is necessary also for the religions to change themselves in order to meet this new need. The time has passed in which God could simply impose Himself on us from without, as master and owner of the estate. Henceforth the world will only kneel before the organic centre of its evolution.

What we are all more or less lacking at this moment is a new definition of holiness.

CONCLUSION

As we said at the beginning, if the interpretation of the phenomenon of spirit here presented is correct, its truth can only be established by the greater coherence it establishes in our perspectives. To see more clearly into the past, and foresee the future in better outline. Now is this not just the result we have attained? To situate the stuff of the universe in consciousness, and to see in the development of this same consciousness the essential fact of nature, seems the only way not only of satisfactorily explaining the present and past aspects of the world around us, but also of organizing the hesitant energies of the earth in view of a possible future. And this seems to be the outcome of our analyses.

a In the first place, only our hypothesis of a cosmos 'in spiritual transformation' explains the features and behaviour of the world around us. The problem of the world, for our minds, is the association it presents of two opposed elements (spirit and matter) in a series of linked combinations covering the expanse between thought and consciousness. Now if consciousness is taken to be a meta-phenomenon this dualism in motion is simply and verbally noted, without any attempt or even any possibility of interpre-

[1]The author was to explain later, in the autobiographical pages entitled *Le cœur de la matière*, how the universe became adorable in his eyes in the person of the Son of God, who assimilated it totally to himself as a result of the Incarnation. (*Ed.*)

tation. If this dualism is pushed aside as an epi-phenomenon, it is conjured out of sight. But it is simply and harmoniously resolved, on the other hand, in a world in which consciousness and its appearance are regarded as *the* phenomenon.[1] Every thing then takes its natural place in a universe in process of changing its spiritual state. Beneath the superficial veil of mechanical processes thrown over it by the laws of great numbers, matter shows itself to be a swarming of elementary consciousness ready to enter into the higher combinations of the organic world. By this fact it ceases to be irreducible to life, the first appearance of which on earth simply corresponds to an emergence of the spontaneous individual into the field of our experience from the inorganic mass. And hominization merely marks a decisive and critical point in the gradual development of this change of state. Evil itself, in all its physical and moral forms, is no longer an intolerable affront to our reason; it is explicable as the residual disorder inevitably mixed with the order which is taking shape in us; and it is justified as the resistance that every synthesis meets, proportional to its sublimity, in realizing itself.

b Only as a result of this does the idea of a cosmos moving towards personality appear capable of sustaining the present energies of humanity and canalizing them towards the future. If one thing is patent today, it is the powerlessness of moralities of balance to govern the earth. In vain do wise men attempt to maintain social and international order by the limitation of force. By the very logic of life force irresistibly arises from everywhere, under our feet and between our hands; and it imperiously re-

[1]This priority ascribed to consciousness and love in the evolution of the phenomenon of the universe is in harmony with the Pauline revelation which proclaims the raising of matter to spirit and of the natural to the supernatural as the principal aim of creation: '*Before the world was made*, he chose us, chose us in Christ, to be holy and spotless, and to live through love in his presence, determining that we should become his adopted sons, through Jesus Christ.' (Eph. 1, 4-5) 'The first-born *of all creation*, for in him *were created all things*.' (Col. 1, 15-16) The version used for these quotations is the Jerusalem Bible. (*Ed.*)

quires to grow to its full. Our world entered the era of force at the same time as it awoke to consciousness of its evolution. It will collapse on itself if it does not discover as a way out some point of convergence above and ahead for its excess of power. It will no longer obey any morality but one of movement; and I cannot conceive of any such morality outside belief in the existence of a transformation which will bring the universe from the material to the spiritual state.

Capable and alone capable either of explaining the past or preserving the future of the type of experimental evolution observed in nature, the theory here proposed of the phenomenon of spirit definitely appears as *true* as any large scale physical hypothesis can be.

But there is more to say. From this first broadly provisional 'truth' flows the possibility of a further proof obtained by direct observation. If it is true, as we have been led to imagine, that cosmic developments of consciousness depend on the existence of a higher and independent centre of personality, there must be a means, without leaving the empirical field, of recognizing around us, in the personalized zones of the universe, some psychic effect (radiation or attraction) specifically connected with the operation of this centre, and consequently revealing its positive existence.

The definitive discovery of the phenomenon of spirit is bound up with the analysis (which science will one day finally undertake) of the 'mystical phenomenon', that is of the love of God.

Unpublished, Pacific, March 1937.

HUMAN ENERGY

As the result of a very natural psychological illusion, our great modern science was born and developed under the exclusive sign of objectivity. Examining matter and life, physicists and biologists have always worked as if they had emerged from and were independent of the world whose elements and laws they were trying to ascertain. Long ago Kant (and in fact the Scholastics before him) pointed to the connexions which make the perceiver and the perceived indissolubly one within the universe. But this fundamental condition of knowledge only perturbed the rare and somewhat unapproachable adepts of metaphysics. For investigators of nature, it seemed indisputably established that things are projected for us 'just as they are' on a screen where we can look at them without being mixed up in them. Scientists contemplated the cosmos without suspecting that they could be influencing it in any degree by the contact of their thought or their senses, without even being aware of belonging intrinsically to the system which they were analysing with such wonder.

Man on one side, the world on the other.

It seems that, for decisive and interior reasons, we are today beginning to emerge from this naïve extrinsicality. On the one hand the objectivity of physicists, pushed to its extremes in breadth and depth, is now tending to reverse. Not only does the disturbing effect of the observer on the thing observed appear on the lower frontier of the experimentable in the realm of material phenomena. But also, taking the construction of waves and particles set up by science over its whole extent, it is becoming clear

113

that this fine edifice contains as much of 'ourselves' as of the 'other'. When they reach a certain degree of breadth and subtlety, the theories of modern physics distinctly reveal the intellectual texture of the investigator's mind beneath the shifting pattern of his phenomena. Hence the suspicion that photons, protons, electrons and other elements of matter have no more (and no less) reality outside our thought than colours independent of our eyes. The old realism of the laboratories veers therefore, by the very logic of its development, towards a scientific idealism: matter being malleable by the intelligence that informs it.

Now, on the other side, that is to say in the territory of biology, a parallel drift is also taking place. It is a curious fact that when, during last century, natural scientists discovered the evolutionary links that connect the elements of the biosphere, they do not seem to have suspected that they had caught themselves in the net that they had just thrown over life. By their own confession, evolution extended to man. And yet in their view man (true man, considered in the development of his thought and social organizations) remained isolated and apart, a spectator not an actor in evolution. But now by way of economic growth and popular uprisings, the neglected element is beginning seriously to invade the field of major experiment and to usurp a place before science. What are the greatest achievements of life in the past compared with the tide of modern civilization? What eruption is comparable to the human explosion? Willingly or unwillingly, we must certainly open a new chapter in the theory of the world: that of the 'phenomenon of man'.

And so in this universe, which we flatter ourselves on regarding from outside 'like gods', we find ourselves immersed, or to be more exact so thoroughly incorporated, that we cannot possibly do or understand anything without apprehending ourselves. In the two realms of matter and life, hitherto the centre of the whole of experience (looking but not looked at), man tends to take up his position as the focal point of our investigations and discoveries. By division and reflexion, the subject of yesterday is about to become the principal object of tomorrow. A little longer, and a *science of man* will have replaced what was hitherto only human science.

I will try in the following pages to call attention to this new orientation, by tracing in broad outline a human energetics.

I THE NATURE AND DIMENSIONS OF HUMAN ENERGY

A Elementary Human Energy: The Human Nucleus

By the energy of man I here mean the always increasing portion of cosmic energy at present undergoing the recognizable influence of the centres of human activity.

In the elementary state (that is to say considered within and around an isolated human element) this 'hominized' energy appears in three forms, at first sight diverse, which it is interesting to distinguish, at least for convenience' sake: incorporated energy, controlled energy, spiritualized energy.

a Incorporated energy is that which the slow biological evolution of the earth has gradually accumulated and harmonized in our organism of flesh and nerves: the astonishing 'natural machine' of the human body.

b Controlled energy is the energy around him which man ingeniously succeeds in dominating with physical power originating from his limbs by means of 'artificial machines.'

c Spiritualized energy, lastly, is localized in the immanent zones of our free activity, and forms the stuff of our intellectual processes, affections and volitions. This energy is probably incapable of measurement, but is very real all the same, since it gains a reflective and passionate mastery of things and their relationships.

These three types of energy, as I said, seem at first sight to form heterogeneous categories. In reality, it appears difficult on reflexion to find a sharp boundary between them. On the one hand, as Bergson observed, it is principally by convention that we distinguish the natural from the artificial. What is in fact, from a profound biological point of view, the difference between the machine formed by a limb and the machine obtained by the artificial extension of that limb, between a bird's wing and an aeroplane's? On the other hand, if spiritual energy, in contrast to incorporated and controlled energies, overflows and overrides the bounds of the physico-chemical, who will doubt that it also contains them? Whence otherwise would it derive its power of animating bodies and its close links with the general state of the world at a given moment?

By all appearances, in fact, every human individual seems to represent a cosmic nucleus of a special nature, radiating around it waves of organization and excitation within matter. Just such a nucleus, with its halo of animation around it, is the unit of human energy.

B Total Human Energy: The Noosphere

Let us now consider human energy as a whole.

This energy is created at every moment by the sum of all the elementary energies accumulated on the earth's surface. Is it possible to imagine it?

As regards the two energies, 'incorporated' and 'controlled', measurement of the kind already practised in other realms of life by scientists like Vernadsky might be theoretically possible. It would be enough to reckon the quantity of organic and inorganic material present in human bodies or in industrial machinery, and calculate what this sum represents in energy accumulated or spent: a matter of statistics. By assessing from moment to moment the percentage of terrestrial energy effectively hominized, this calculation would allow us to appreciate the size and gradient of the phenomenon of man in its most external zone.

The measurement of spiritualized energy presents far more difficulties. It is no doubt not improbable that science will one day, by means of chemical quantitative analyses or by the discovery of some vital radiation, succeed in measuring the power released in the course of psychic events. But even if this measurement of nervous energy were to be achieved, it would by no means represent the breadth and riches of the world of ideas and affections, of which the energy of man ultimately consists. In order to gain some idea of its inner dimensions, we could hardly resort to any but indirect considerations, some based on the number of human particles, others on the links between them.

The number, first of all. Human plurality is in some respects a great weakness, in others an extraordinary strength. A variety of complementary points of view, a multiplicity of groping efforts, of searching antennae: this is how our state of multiplicity, which in other connexions causes us such suffering, appears from the point of view of energetics. Have we ever tried to imagine the thousand million human units exerting at every moment intellectual pressure on the universe?

But, viewed on the cosmic scale, these numbers alone are of very little account. Of what importance is the human population of the globe compared with the myriads of particles contained in a drop of water? The truly impressive aspect of total human energy only appears when we decide to observe it from the point of view of its inner connexions. In fact elementary human energies do not operate in disorder, in obedience to merely statistical laws. Nor do they vibrate only in a well defined common direction, of which we shall have to speak later: simply in the direction of greatest consciousness. There is more to it than that. They tend to combine their individual radiations in a single pulsation, that is to say to constitute an organized whole. Until we have perceived this, we shall understand nothing about the problem of human energy.

This fundamental connexion of the living world is not immediately perceptible. Particles swamped amidst other particles, we live habitually unaware of what the mass of consciousness of which we form a part must represent, viewed as a whole. We are like a cell which can see nothing but other cells in the body to which it belongs. And yet the body exists more than the elements of which it is composed. In fact we can expect no decisive advance in our conceptions of the animate world for so long as we remain on the 'cellular' scale and are unable to mount above living beings to see life, above men to discover humanity: not that abstract and suffering humanity of which the philanthropists speak but the living and powerful reality in which all the thoughts of individuals are steeped, and by which they are guided to form from their linked multiplicity a single spirit of the earth.

This perception of a natural psychic unity higher than our 'souls'[1] requires, as I know from experience, a special quality and training in the observer. Like all broad scientific perspectives it is the product of a prolonged reflexion, leading to the discovery of a deep cosmic sense in connexions which habit has accustomed us to regard as superficial, banal, and in fact moral. It is not much easier to see the humanity I am speaking of than to take up a position in the world of relativity. But once we manage to affect this change of viewpoint, then the earth, our little human earth, is draped in splendour. Floating above the biosphere, whose layers no doubt gradually merge into it, the world of thought, the noosphere, begins to let its crown shine.

The noosphere!

It is to this magnitude, and to this magnitude alone, that the considerations on human energy which follow ultimately apply. It will be useless for those who cannot see it to follow me further.

II SIGNIFICANCE AND VALUE OF HUMAN ENERGY

Even taken in its full grandeur, and the totality of its interconnexions which make it a natural unity of planetary dimensions, human energy might seem of no account, lost amidst the fantastic sidereal energies in which it is immersed, if it did not show itself to be invested with certain particular qualities.

[1] Our individual psychism. (*Ed.*)

These qualities can be recognized and confirmed by a simple consideration of the value which thought assumes, if contrasted with the crude powers of matter. These only appear with complete clarity in the perspective of duration, that is to say of evolution.

I will not repeat in detail arguments that I have many times developed elsewhere. But I must at least sketch their main outline. This can be set out in the following thesis: 'By the simple fact of his presence in nature, man imposes on the cosmos, first a *certain stuff* and then a *certain structure*; and the result of this dual operation is to make him, man, *the most significant and the most valuable portion of the universe* in the field of our experience.'

Let us study the three terms of this proposition in succession. A certain stuff, first of all. For obvious reasons of intellectual and practical convenience, science has always tried, from its beginnings, to explain the world (that is to say to give it a coherent total pattern) with matter as its starting point. Now in this effort of synthesis it has more and more palpably come up against an insurmountable obstacle: life. We must indeed bow to the facts. *Taken on the ascending scale*, starting from mechanical determinisms, life appears to the physical scientist as a series of unclimbable steps. The animals, and more especially man, in whom the phenomena of spontaneity and immanence definitely emerge, cannot possibly be integrated into a purely mechanistic natural system. But it would be impossible to leave them out of our picture; this omission would prove science bankrupt. How do we get out of the quandary? A single way out presents itself: to reverse direction. Hitherto we have tried to attain and reproduce spirit by approaching it from matter. Now our task is to rejoin and reconstitute matter by an opposite process, by coming down from spirit accepted as the primal substance of things. Let us assume as an axiom that only spontaneity and consciousness (masked though they may be by a state of extreme division and diffusion) exist at the beginning. Then the determinisms which we chose to consider as essential to the world would be no more than an inelastic veil cast over a mass of elementary freedoms by the play of great numbers. If we follow this line, the difficulties disappear; the road becomes level, and movement becomes possible between the two poles of the universe, the conscious and the unconscious. If the cosmos were basically material, it would be physically incapable of containing man. Therefore, we may conclude (and this is the first step) that it is in its inner being made *of spiritual stuff*.

And now (we have reached the second step) what must be the texture of this cosmic spiritual stuff that will allow man, now possible in nature, effectively to occupy the special position in the system of things that experience reveals?

If there is one discovery to which the most certain findings of 'positional' biology lead, it is undoubtedly:

a that the spiritual (that is to say the elements constituting the biosphere) are disposed radially around man;

b this radial distribution depending not on a simple effect of perspective (as in the case of the features of landscape) but on a natural distribution of living beings;

c this distribution, in its turn, not being due to some static grouping or ordering but resulting from a gradual establishment.

In other words, starting from man as the centre, spirituality manifestly diminishes in steps around as well as behind us. What can be the significance of this phenomenon?

Only one interpretation seems capable of accounting for all these different appearances at once. And this is to admit that the spiritual layers of the universe have undergone a joint movement, drawing them towards a growing concentration of the quantity of consciousness which they contain. The appearance of the firmament would be unintelligible to the astronomer without the gyration of the nebular masses. The texture of a twig would be inexplicable without the development of the plant. Likewise, man's position in nature cannot be explained without a factor of psychic growth. No, the universe was not born without motion;

its structure betrays (at least in the past) a global evolution of its mass towards an ever increasing interiorization, leading finally to reflexion.

On this assumption, the conclusion we announced becomes automatically clear. Being in the forefront of the cosmic wave of advance, the energy of man assumes an importance disproportionate to its apparently small size. Compared with the magnitude of the stars, the noosphere is an almost insignificant film. In reality this thin surface is nothing less than the most progressive form under which it has been given to us to apprehend and contemplate the energy of the universe. This tenuous envelope holds the secret essence of the vastnesses that it fringes: the highest note reached by the vibration of worlds.

The meaning of this is twofold:

First, that the *direction* of advance so far followed by the cosmos is indicated to us by the human spearhead. Consequently, by analysing the conditions of our activity, we can hope to discover the fundamental conditions which govern the general functioning of the universe.

Second, that in *magnitude* we hold, concentrated in the human mass, the most living, quintessential treasure and hope of the world.

What must we and what can we do with it?

This question, on which the whole application of our freedom depends, can only be resolved by a look forward.

III THE FUTURE AND PROBLEM OF HUMAN ENERGY

The energy of man, as we have just recognized, comes to our notice as the last factor of a vast process in which the total mass of the universe is engaged. But here two alternative possibilities face us. Has this process attained a state of equilibrium, or is it still developing? Does the noosphere represent a sort of stationary wave in which the spiritualized energy of our world is consumed and perfected at every moment, leaving nothing over? Or, on the other hand, is it animated by a movement of its own, drawing it towards concentration, that is to say towards a spiritualization of a higher order? More simply, has evolution stopped with and in man? Or does it continue through him, further, beyond ourselves?

To so-called 'commonsensical' minds the idea of a general drift of man towards some state of super-humanity seems improbable or even absurd. 'How do we differ from our ancestors', they ask, 'except by our greater faults and a sort of trend to decadence? Were not the Egyptians, the Greeks and the people of the Middle Ages our equals or even our superiors?' Thus speak the men 'of good sense', forgetting that for the past century science has continuously contradicted the kind of evidence on which they are relying. One after another, the most reliable foundations of the universe have shown themselves to be subject to currents all the broader and more powerful the more immovable their basis might seem. The law seems categorical: the more considerable the portion of the universe a movement affects, the slower its rhythm. Despite their apparent fixity the stellar systems alter, the stars have a life-cycle, the continents shift, mountains arise, animal species are transformed. All these changes, insensible in relation to the length of a human existence, are going on at this very moment all around us. *Why should the most essential current of life alone be static?* No scientist today doubts that humanity appeared as the result of evolution. By what improbable exception to the general conditions of the universe could this evolution by which we were born have become stationary?

To anyone familiar with the behaviour of the 'immense', observed over a very large slice of time, the idea of a human super-development, far from seeming strange, must seem entirely credible. Now this simple theoretical probability is rapidly confirmed by a variety of indications which strike his attention. To a geologist tiny particulars (a fragment of terrain recently uplifted, a seismic disturbance) demonstrate the continued vitality of a

Himalaya. In the same way, to a mind alert to a possible movement of the noosphere, a whole series of facts generally considered negligible or ambiguous becomes significant.

To take the history of humanity in a first broad sweep, the sudden appearance of art in the caves, agricultural society replacing hunting and food-gathering, and finally the intellectual and economic revolution which produced our modern age, cease to be indifferent accidents, and take the appearance of successive stages or pulsations, following one another along an axis of movement.

More detailed and closer to us, the astonishing connexions established beneath our eyes by way of the air and the ether, the discovery of time and space, the exploration of the infinitely small and the infinitely great, and totalitarian social movements suddenly assume a strange relief. None of them are regarded by any of our contemporaries as anything but superficial ameliorations or tiresome crises, or curious events in the earth's history. But do not these advances on the contrary mark perfectly direct expansions and adaptations in the three parts (incorporated, controlled and spiritualized) of human energy? A humanity grown capable of consciously assuming its place in cosmic evolution and pulsating as a whole (with its own wave-length, I would venture to say) with a common emotion—a humanity of this sort, whatever its residual imperfections and the crises connected with its metamorphosis, is surely now, in comparison with the neolithic world, organically a true super-humanity.

Finally let us consider the question of unemployment, which is so serious today. It is usual to curse it, to accuse the machine of causing it or, which is partially true, to lay the blame on the bad economic organization of the world. But such criticisms do not find or reach the root of the matter. Considered from the evolutionary point of view, unemployment can be defined as the sudden appearance of a mass of human energy violently released by an internal adjustment of the noosphere. The phenomenon creates its own danger. It calls for its own remedies. But just as inevitably (and beneficially) as the advance of the universe, it manifests with singular clarity, for anyone with eyes to see, the reality of that advance itself.

The alternative presented at the opening of this section seems finally to resolve itself in favour of a continuation of the evolutionary movement within humanity. And here we are confronted with the following physical perspective. Around us and in us the energy of man, itself sustained by the energy of the universe of which it is the crown, is still pursuing its mysterious progress towards higher states of thought and freedom. Willy-nilly, we are totally caught up in this transformation. I repeat my question, therefore: What shall we do? Resist the current? This would be foolish and moreover impossible. Let ourselves be passively carried along by the wave? This would be cowardice. And anyhow, how can we remain neutral, since our essence is to act? Only one way remains open to us: to trust in the infallibility and finally beatifying value of the action in which we are involved. In us the world's evolution towards spirit has become conscious. Our perfection, our interest, our salvation as elements can depend therefore on nothing less than pushing this evolution forward with all our strength. We may not yet understand exactly where it is taking us, but it is absurd for us to doubt that it is leading us towards some end of supreme value.

Hence it is that, *for the first time* since the awakening of life on earth, the fundamental problem of action has finally emerged into our human consciousness in the twentieth century. Up to now man has acted principally out of instinct, from day to day, without much knowledge of why or for whom he was working. Contemporaneously with the flowing into him of fresh powers, a new limitless and immeasurable field of activity is opened for his ambitions and, in some sense, for his worship. For anyone who has understood (and everyone will inevitably do so soon) the position and significance of the smallest portion of thought in nature, the fundamental matter has become one of rationally assuring the progress of the world of which we form part. No longer only, as of old, for our little individuality, our little family, our little country—no longer indeed only for the whole earth —but for the salvation and success of the universe itself, how should we modern men best organize the maintenance, distribution and progress of the energy of man around us?

Therein lies the whole question.

IV THE CONSCIOUS ORGANIZATION OF HUMAN ENERGY

Under the combined influence of the most recent material progress and the present social crises, the idea of envisaging and scientifically treating the energy of humanity 'as a whole' is just emerging from the zone of speculations and dreams. Physiologists like Doctor Carrel, biologists and even men of letters like the two Huxleys, allied with engineers and economists in the 'Centre for the Study of Human Problems'[1] inspired by Jean Coutrot, join independently with metaphysicians like Bergson to lay the foundations of a science (theoretical and practical at once) of human activity, which already promises to be the great science of tomorrow. The organization of the spirit following on that of matter.

It could not possibly be my business here to present a detailed programme for this new discipline and technique. On the other hand it falls within my subject to sketch its possible form in order by this example to give a more concrete meaning to what we can call human energetics.

But first, two preliminary remarks on which the whole sequel of our argument depends.

First, from the standpoint we have adopted, it is clear that there is no essential difference between what we commonly distinguish by the two names of physical energy and moral power.[2] If, as we believe we have established, the cosmos is of spiritual stuff, then a

[1] Le centre d'étude des problèmes humains.
[2] In their character of natural (and not artificial) reality. (*Ed.*)

mechanical assemblage artificially obtained, an attraction of an affective nature, progress in economic and social organization, a link by Hertzian waves, even an intellectual systematization have as much *physical* reality as corpuscular attractions and groupings or natural connexions forming organic bodies. Perhaps they have even more. In the cosmos that has revealed itself to our eyes there is no longer any fundamental distinction to be made between the physical and the moral. The domain of human energy is the 'physico-moral.'

Second general observation. Under whatever particular form it is considered, the physico-moral obeys in its activity a double law, both essential and universal: *to try everything—to its conclusion.* Like the molecules of a gas, the innumerable human units press simultaneously on the entire surface of the obstacles opposing their expansion, until they are either overcome or circumvented at their point of least resistance. And when by groping an issue is found, their mass tends to rush out through it until it is completely exhausted. This accords with the corpuscular structure and internal tension that characterize the noosphere. When therefore, later in this essay, we come to discuss the pursuit of some result in the field of human energy, it will always be understood that the effort under consideration must be made by means of an infinite number of successive attempts until the maximum realization of the desired effect has been obtained. To try everything, for the sake of ever increasing knowledge and power: this is the most general formula and the highest law of human activity and morality.

Having accepted this, we can directly approach the problem we have set ourselves. How are we to imagine the rational organization of the energy contained in our noosphere?

A Organization of Elementary Human Energy: Personalism

The first object that should arouse the attention of a specialist in human energy is to assure the human nuclei taken in isolation their maximum of elementary solidity and 'efficiency'. To perfect individuals so as to confer on the group its maximum of power: this is the obvious course to follow for the final success of the operation.

On a rough view, the improvement of the human particles appears realizable by means of a certain number of *general* measures valid for all the particles *of whatever kind*. Let us view it in the three realms of incorporated, controlled and spiritualized energy in turn.

a As regards elementary incorporated or organic energy, an immense task (undertaken already of course but without any general idea) is offered to biology, physiology and medicine: not only the scientific conquest of disease and the phenomena of counter-evolution (sterility, physical deterioration) which undermine the advances of the noosphere; but to release by various methods (selection, balance of the sexes, action of hormones, hygiene, etc.) a higher human type. Such an ambition has long appeared, and still appears to many, fantastic or even blasphemous. Some refuse to imagine any profound change in what seems 'to have always been'; others have a false religious fear of violating the Creator's irrevocable rights over His work both of flesh and thought. For a complex of obscure reasons, our generation still regards with distrust all efforts proposed by science for controlling the machinery of heredity, of sex-determination and development of the nervous system. It is as if man had the right and power to interfere with all the channels in the world except those which make him himself. And yet it is eminently on this ground that we must try *everything*, to its conclusion. A delicate undertaking, if ever there was one; but precisely because of their delicacy, these undertakings require, if they are to be soundly, reverently and religiously pursued, the precautions and surveyance of methodically conducted research. No longer only man experimenting on his fellows; but humanity feeling out in order to give its members a higher quality of life. Novelists like H. G. Wells and Aldous Huxley have tried, somewhat satirically, to draw a possible picture of such attempts and their results. Let us hold to the idea without letting ourselves be put out by their pictures. The idea is right and grand, and its realization, like all life's actions, will defy caricature.

b In the field of controlled energy, by definition the efforts of the new techniques must on the one hand tend increasingly to strengthen by appropriate measures (aeroplanes, radios, 'movies') the ray of penetration, action and therefore connexion belonging to each human element; and on the other hand to make available, by a judicious use of automatic machinery, an ever increasing portion of the activities contained in that element. We already know the effects. But do we ever dream of their incalculable developments and reverberations? In the first place, multiplied by the number of individuals affected, each advance in either direction is necessarily destined to be translated into a positive forward-leap in the curve of total human energy. Moreover, in both cases, the final result is of supreme importance. Whether as a result of expansion or liberation, each advance that man makes in the mechanization of the world overflows the plane of matter. For it adds to the new possibilities arising from the improvements made on organic matter and this produces an increase of spiritual energy in the individual.

c Spiritualized energy, as we have seen, is the flower of cosmic energy. It is consequently the most interesting part of human energy for organization. In what principal direction can we expect it to extend in our individual natures, and in what way can we aid it to do so? We must undoubtedly reply in the direction of a decisive expansion of certain of our ancient powers, reinforced by the acquisition of certain new faculties or consciousnesses.

Expansion or even metamorphosis of certain ancient powers. For the last century, without greatly noticing it, we have been undergoing a remarkable transformation in the range of intellect. To discover and know has always been a deep tendency of our nature. Can we not recognize it already in cave man? But it is only yesterday that this essential need to know has become explicit and changed into a vital autonomous function, taking precedence in our lives over our preoccupation with food and drink. Now, if I am not mistaken, this phenomenon of the individualization of our highest psychological functions is not only far from having reached its limits in the field of pure thought, but is also tending to develop in a neighbouring realm, which has remained practically undefined and unexplored: the 'terra ignota' of the affections and love.

Paradoxically, love (I understand love here in the strict sense of 'passion'), despite (or perhaps precisely because of) its ubiquity and violence, has hitherto been excluded from any rational systematization of the energy of man. Empirically, morality has succeeded more or less successfully in codifying its practice with a view to the maintenance and material propagation of the race. But has anyone seriously thought that beneath this turbulent power (which is nevertheless well known to be the inspirer of genius, the arts and all poetry), a formidable creative urge has remained in reserve, and that man will only be truly man from the day when he has not only checked, but transformed, utilized and liberated it? Today, for our century, avid to lose no energy and to control the most intimate psychological mechanism, light seems to be beginning to break. Love, like thought, is still in full growth in the noosphere. The excess of its growing energies over the daily diminishing needs of human propagation becomes every day more manifest. And love is therefore tending in a purely hominized form to fill a much larger function than the simple urge to reproduction. Between man and woman a specific and mutual power of spiritual sensitization and fertilization is probably still slumbering. It demands to be released, so that it may flow irresistibly towards the true and beautiful. Its awakening is certain. Expansion, I have said, of an ancient power. The expression is undoubtedly too weak. Beyond a certain degree of sublimation spiritualized love, by the boundless possibilities of intuition and communication it contains, penetrates the unknown; it will in our sight take its place, in the mysterious future, with the group of new faculties and consciousnesses that is awaiting us.

New faculties and consciousnesses. By this I do not simply mean the artificial extension of our senses to additional radiations, marvellous though this is: infinite rumours suddenly filling a sphere of melancholy silence, as it has for our generation; I am thinking of more direct modes of perception and action, coming, in fulfilment of very old hopes, to show that matter is transparent and malleable in relation to spirit. Men have for long been seeking a means of immediately influencing the bodies and souls around them by their will, and of penetrating them by a direct vision. Their random attempts, made without any controlling idea or general method, have so far failed. But tomorrow they may succeed. Conforming to recent views which point towards the idea of a spiritual essence of matter, physics will surely isolate and master the secret that lies at the heart of metapsychics. And even if physics does not succeed in this task, which perhaps does not lie in its realm, will not certain psychological effects of another order (I am thinking here of 'mysticism') one day secure our bodies' long-dreamed escape from their determinisms and our souls' release from their isolation? If there is any premonitory sign of this profound metamorphosis, it is doubtless the formation at present taking place in our modern consciousnesses of a special sense for seeing the totality in which alone the miracle of our liberation and mutual penetration (or transparency) can take place. Pantheistic aspirations towards a universal communion are as old in man as his 'spiritualistic' attempts to conquer matter. But only lately, thanks to the precise data provided by science concerning the unity of matter and energy and the reality of a cosmogenesis, have these vague desires begun to take the rational form of definite intellectual discoveries. In every realm we are beginning habitually to live in the presence of the All and with some attention to it. Nothing seems to me more vital, from the point of view of human energy, than the spontaneous appearance and, eventually, the systematic cultivation of such a 'cosmic sense'. It is raising men to the explicit perception of their 'molecular' nature. They are ceasing to be closed individuals, to become parts. From now on elementary spiritual energy is definitely ready in them to be integrated in the total energy of the noosphere.

But before undertaking the study of this last energy, let us not fail to bring out an important point. In the course of the preceding remarks we have deliberately limited ourselves to the consideration of the *general* lines along which a progress of motivational human nature taken *in genere* may be anticipated. Now this approximation must not make us forget the essential and final point of the *individual quality* of individuals. In virtue of the spiritual nature of the noosphere, its elements are not exactly comparable with the anonymous and interchangeable corpuscles of a gaseous mass. They correspond rather to the cells of a highly specialized organism, each of which occupies and is alone capable of occupying a fixed place. This means that the perfection and utility of each nucleus of human energy in relation to the whole, definitely depend on what is unique and incommunicable in the achievement of each. The final preoccupation of any specialist in spirit, therefore, when dealing with human units who are undergoing any kind of transformation under his direction, is to leave them the possibility of self-discovery and the freedom of self-differentiation, both to an ever-increasing extent.

The organization of elementary human energy, whatever its generalized methods, must culminate in the formation, within each element, *of a maximum of personality*.

B Organization of Total Human Energy: The Common Human Soul

The true problem of human energy lies in its *total* technical utilization. For a long time this problem necessarily remained unnoticed, since it could not be formulated till, thanks to scientific syntheses and social relationships, the dynamic unity of the noosphere was present in our minds. But today when the gathering of the human layer is taking place before our eyes, its reality decidedly enters the field of common observation. A proof, if ever there was one, that man, supposing him to be henceforth fixed in his individual nature, sees a new and boundless field of evolution opening before him: the realm of collective creation, associations, ideas and emotions. How can we fix limits on the effects of expansion, penetration and spiritual fusion, resulting from a coherent adjustment of the human multitude? It is something to master and canalize the powers of the ether and the sea. But what is that triumph compared with the global mastery of human thought and human love? Never indeed was a more magnificent opportunity offered to the hopes and endeavours of the earth.

Considered along its principal axes, the organization of total human energy is fairly easy to define, at least in its beginnings. At the majority of the affected points the movement has spontaneously started under the material pressure of current events. Consequently the work of technicians in this realm consists less perhaps in imagining new ways of advance than in recognizing the significance and guessing the logical extensions of processes that are already under way.

a In the matter of 'incorporated' energy we are incredibly slow to achieve (or even to conceive) the realization of a 'body' of humanity. In this field the apostles of birth control (although too often inspired by the narrow desire of relieving individual hardships) will have rendered us the service of opening our eyes to the anomaly of a society that concerns itself with everything except the recruitment of its own elements. Now eugenics does not confine itself to a simple control of births. All sorts of related questions, scarcely yet raised despite their urgency, are attached to it. What fundamental attitude, for example, should the advancing wing of humanity take to fixed or definitely unprogressive ethnical groups? The earth is a closed and limited surface. To what extent should it tolerate, racially or nationally, areas of lesser activity? More generally still, how should we judge the efforts we lavish in all kinds of hospitals on saving what is so often no more than one of life's rejects? Something profoundly true and beautiful (I mean faith in the irreplaceable value and unpredictable resources contained in each personal unit) is evidently concealed in persistent sacrifice to save a human existence. But should not this solicitude of man for his individual neighbour be balanced by a higher passion, born of the faith in that other higher personality that is to be expected, as we shall see, from the worldwide achievements of our evolution? To what extent should not the development of the strong (to the extent that we can define this quality) take precedence over the preservation of the weak? How can we reconcile, in a state of maximum efficiency, the care lavished on the wounded with the more urgent necessities of battle?[1] In what does true charity consist?

So many problems the solution of which can only be approached by previously fixing, on a very broad basis, a scale and plan of distribution of human values. How are we to sort and distribute materials without first deciding what we have to build?

b In the field of 'controlled' energies, we seem better able to distinguish our methods of construction. The adjustment of the mechanisms of which the greater human body is artificially constructed does not in fact raise the same delicate problems as the direct manipulation of living organisms.

In this realm one first precaution of the new technics must clearly be to make sure of growing supplies of usable material energy. After coal, water, oil, what next? On this point we can put our trust in physics. But considering the rate at which we are using up our reserves, we must hasten to find something else. And we have nothing else yet. Seemingly, no less urgent than the question of sources of energy is the world-wide installation of a general economy of production and labour, reinforced by the establishment of a rational gold policy. Financial and social crises

[1]Teilhard's constant efforts both to encourage the weak and inspire the strong prove that he knew how to make this reconciliation. (Ed.)

are at pains to remind us how confused our theories are in these matters and how barbarous our conduct. But when will men decide to recognize that no serious progress can be made in these directions except under two conditions: first that the proposed organization must be international and in the end totalitarian[1]; and secondly that it must be conceived on a very large scale. What is ruining our present day economics and politics is not only their persistent segmentation of the world into tight compartments. More lethal still is their stubborn conservation of a static form and ideal: reciprocal areas of exchange whose perfection it seems would consist in a private short circuit. In contradiction to this doctrine of closed equilibrium, a general theory of human energy must bring out the necessity of an essential supporting of our earthly activities on the future. Irresistibly, the noosphere is internally accumulating an ever increasing tension. We are bursting with power, or rather it is driving us to crush one another. We try to cure ourselves of these troubles by limitation of force. An impossible and also an immoral course. Our cure lies in the discovery of a natural and productive way of passing on the superabundance that oppresses us. An ever greater excess of free energy available for ever vaster conquests: this is what the world expects of us, and this is what will save us.

Now there is no lack of objectives on which we can reasonably divert this natural excess of power: vast areas to be developed and made habitable, an organized struggle against disease, collective projects of exploration and research. Let us stress this last point. It seems to me to contain the final solution of problems presented by the utilization of human energy.

We are pleased to pride ourselves on living in an enlightened and scientific century. And yet the truth is, on the contrary, that we still drag on with rudimentary and childish forms of intellectual advance. A scientific century, we have said. But what is the proportion of our terrestrial resources—in money, men and

[1]Obviously this adjective is intended to convey a general notion of totality, not a so-called 'totalitarian' regime. (Ed.)

organization—at present employed in visiting and conquering the still unknown tracts of the world? If we attempt the calculation, we shall be surprised at the tiny percentage that is involved. Some millionths of our total energy perhaps. Hardly the price of a crew of a battleship. This is a crude fact: research (a function which everyone agrees to be of the highest value in the world) is still for the most part left to the unordered endeavours of a few volunteers or private institutions. This state of things is simply a biological scandal. Not only does our negligence and disorder impose a serious brake on the speed of development, but so long as they last, we shall have to abandon all real hope of certain—and probably the most important—discoveries, of which we stand in need. No field or laboratory worker will contradict me here. We have now reached the limit of progress realizable by *individual* efforts. Science is waiting for us to pursue it on an industrial scale. Without means of this sort, it will lack proper foundations. To try everything to its conclusion. This formula will only become a reality when scientific experiment is organized not merely on a national scale but on the scale of humanity.

Now what would happen if we were to decide finally to concentrate the point of our ambitions on this pole of discovery? Neither more nor less than this perhaps: that the definite breakthrough would be made for our overflowing powers into a boundless field of expansion and conquest.

At present the majority of men do not yet understand force (the key and symbol of greater-being) except in its most primitive and savage form of war. This is perhaps why it is necessary for us to continue for some time still to manufacture ever greater and more destructive weapons. For we still, alas, need these machines to translate the vital sense of attack and victory into concrete experience. But may the moment come (and it will come) when the masses realize that the true human victories are those over the mysteries of matter and life. May the moment come when the man in the street understands that there is more poetry in a mighty machine for splitting the atom than in any artillery. A decisive hour will strike for man, when the spirit of discovery absorbs the whole vital force contained in the spirit of war. A supreme phase of history in which the whole power of fleets and armies will be transformed, to reinforce that other power which the machine will have rendered idle. Then an irresistible tide of free energies will advance into the most progressive tracts of the noosphere.

An important part of this mass of available energy will immediately be absorbed by man's material expansion. But another portion, the most valuable, will necessarily flow on to the levels of spiritualized energy, with which we must concern ourselves now.

c The possible increases of total spiritual energy derive, strictly speaking, from what Bergson has called 'creative' evolution. They are therefore by nature unpredictable. What will the higher forms of intuition, art and thought be tomorrow? We not only cannot say, but simply cannot imagine. But though we must here forgo any pictured anticipation of the future, we can nevertheless state the general type of advances that can be expected. They will take place, as they have already begun, in the direction and under the domination of a *growing unity*. It is important to be clear about this.

We have devoted much attention in the last few pages to the web of mechanical and social connexions from which the tangible envelope of humanity is being woven before our eyes. Now this increasingly close tissue of material cohesion is only the external indication of another far more fundamental work that is at present taking place: the inner psychical organization of the noosphere. The first step towards this immanent elaboration of total human energy has taken place in the mechanical field under pressure of the most urgent necessities of life. Historical materialism, Marx would say. In order to obtain the results of collective organization and discovery necessary for their subsistence, active thinking units are automatically led to form a linked operational group: a 'front-line' of humanity.

But these first manifestations of a common consciousness possess a living need for inner precision and expansion. *Intellectually*, scientific progress will create a synthesis of the laws of matter and life, which is fundamentally nothing but a collective act of perception: the world seen in a single coherent perspective by humanity as a whole. *Socially* the mingling and melting of races are directly leading to the establishment of an equally common form not only of language, but of morality and ideology. *Affectively*, the community of interest and struggle for common objectives is *ipso facto* accompanied by a comradeship in battle, the natural prototype of *love* or *sense of humanity*. Thus, by all sorts of different ways, what was at first only an almost material grouping for progress and attack tends to assume an inner consistency and to take itself as an autonomous subject for reflexion and action. Under the combined effect of the material needs and spiritual affinities of life, humanity all around us is beginning to emerge from impersonality and assume some sort of heart and face.

With the recording of this mysterious birth, the most general picture so far vouchsafed us of the biological current that is drawing us on is completed and disappears from sight.

The organization of human energy, taken as a whole, is directed and pushes us towards the ultimate formation, over and above each personal element, *of a common soul of humanity*.

V THE MAINTENANCE OF HUMAN ENERGY AND 'THE
COSMIC POINT OMEGA'

Expansion in space and increased depth of spirit. Continuous extension of the radius revealing itself by a continual enrichment of the centre. The more the noosphere by virtue of these two conjoint movements goes on stretching externally and becoming more compact within, the more the power it consumes in its working and the power it absorbs in its syntheses will necessarily increase.

By what mechanism and on what fuel can we imagine, will human energy maintain itself?

Considered in its organic material zones, human energy obeys the laws of physics and draws quite naturally on the reserves of heat available in nature. But studied in its axial, spiritualized form, it is found to be fed by a particular current (of which thermo-dynamics might well be, after all, no more than a statistical echo) which, for want of a better name, we will call 'tension of consciousness'. We are rightly concerned for our terrestrial reserves of combustibles and metals. But do we sufficiently consider that humanity would be miserably extinguished on piles of calories the moment its passion for growth and its appetite for life diminished? In the last resort, when everything has been provided for a rational organization of our world, the earth's technicians are faced with this vital question: 'On what conditions will reflective life, the progress of which we are trying to organize, preserve or even increase (as is necessary) its penetrative force and power of shock?'

It would be idle to evade the difficulty by writing down 'tension of consciousness' as an instinct which will push us blindly forward. Does not the fine point of the human problem lie precisely in explaining how the life-urge may prolong itself by *becoming self-conscious*? It would, in another respect, be insufficient to ascribe our march towards the future to the simple fear of danger and pain. This treading on our heels *a tergo* by material necessities certainly plays a part in the phenomenon of human progress. But it can only be a secondary and subordinate part. Directed principally towards the lesser evil, life takes shelter and grows a shell; it has no need to advance. No, it is not from a desperate effort to *survive*, but by a stubborn will for *greater life* that humanity was born.

We cannot therefore fail to come to the following idea—which coincides moreover with one of the oldest and commonest intuitions of our consciousness: 'the *conspiration*' of activities from which the collective human soul proceeds presumes at its beginning the common '*aspiration*' exerted by a hope. To wake and nourish human energy, there must have been at the very outset an inner attraction towards a desired object. Things cannot have happened otherwise.

To define this hope, to discover this object would be to put one's finger on the ultimate springs of human energy. Let us try to do so, by three successive stages.

At a first approximation, it follows from what we have already said about the birth of a cosmic sense that the prime mover of human activity can only have been a reality possessing *universal dimensions*. No reflective organization would have been possible without the initial choice which made us incline, with heart and mind, towards being rather than non-being. Now this fundamental preference for being, without which the world, as it attained thought, would logically have returned to dust, necessarily implies faith in some final completion of *everything* around us. If being is by nature holy there is no salvation except of *everything* that exists. We act therefore, in the final analysis, in obedience to a world, to incorporate ourselves in a world, to complete ourselves with the world. A total and totalizing end: nothing less could set the springs of our liberty in motion and bend them to it.

More exactly, and still by virtue of the preceding analyses, we are also justified in affirming that the supremely desirable objective, the attraction of which was instrumental in deciding us to collaborate with the universe, *to some extent coincides with the full flowering of human energy itself*. For this energy, as we have recognized, is something very different from a simple *means* of action. It bears within it the product of its own employment. We have been able to define it as an area of transformation and a propagating front for universal energy, but also and better as a *common soul*. On this point, in fact, the advances of modern consciousness have already left the realm of speculation to enter the field of practical attitudes. Not only for an elect minority but for the masses as well, it has become a commonly accepted 'article of faith' that if there is any way forward for the world and salvation for the individual, they await us in the direction of some higher form to be attained by humanity.

But how exactly are we to picture the features of this super-humanity in which the world is to be epitomized? This is the third step in our enquiry.

As regards the future, when we are concerned not with mechanical determinisms but with life, it would be absurd, let me say once more, to 'imagine'. But it is at least possible for us to decide what general conditions the future must satisfy to remain coherent with the present. The features of this whole subject of trans-humanity, which has been in continuous creation throughout the vicissitudes of the earth, perforce escape us. But what must be the *known* attributes of this centre, by what sort of rays already perceived must it influence our souls, in order that its attraction may have the physical virtue of drawing ever higher the increasingly conscious layers of the noosphere? This question inevitably confronts our free minds, and it has certainly an answer, since on that answer depends the maintenance of human energy. Let us look for it.

To a problem of immanent nature the solution can only be found in our own hearts. Like everyone interested in the essentially modern problem of action, I have often examined myself to discover what attributes I seemed psychologically *obliged* to confer on the positive pole of things in order to have courage to submit to its direction. Now I have finally come to the following conclusion. Two conditions are necessary (and in fact sufficient) to make us accept and co-operate with the demands of evolution: the universal and superhuman end to which it is taking us must present itself to us as at the same time *incorruptible* and *personal*. And that it is so I should like to show.

First, incorruptible. Death has been tirelessly examined by man in the partings and humiliations that accompany it. Tirelessly, the moralists have used the power ascribed to it to throw salutary cold water on the fever of our passions. But have we ever sufficiently examined the power it has of lighting the most distant horizons of human energy? Death is probably almost nothing to an animal; absorbed in its actions, it never leaves the present moment. But what proportions does this phenomenon not take when transported into the surroundings of the noosphere? How will the being react, once confronted and for the whole of his life with an end in which he appears to perish completely? Resignation? Stoicism? Not at all, I say, but *legitimate* revolt and desertion, unless death reveals the form or condition of a new progress. To act is to create, and creation is for ever. Reflective action and the expectation of total disappearance are therefore *cosmically incompatible*. The association, therefore, in a single evolutionary current of thought and death raises a fundamental conflict which must end in the destruction of one of these two contradictory ends. Either spirit will see that it has been deceived and retire from the game. Or else death, lifting its veil of annihilation, will take on the features of life. Now the first alternative would involve the absurdity of a universe victorious over unconsciousness as far as man, yet successfully bringing reflexion to birth in him only to show itself, the universe, incapable of sustaining it. There remains the second alternative, that death leaves some part of ourselves existing in some way, to which we can turn with devotion and interest, as to a portion of the absolute. The final fate to which we must be destined by our incorporation in the universe must, *in order to be such*, appear to our hopes as *imperishable*. That, as I have already stated, is a first condition *sine qua non* for the deployment of human energy.

Incorruptibility, therefore. But also, I added, *personality*. Certainly men—I have known several—who have felt the need of finding some extension to our existences try to console themselves for their eventual disappearance with the thought that their ashes will rejoin and disappear in the great stream of matter. Matter in its simplest and most imperishable forms would in that case be the unchangeable environment in which we shall finally rest. A moment's reflection is enough to show the disadvantage of this prospect. Elementary matter might, it is supposed, represent the form of equilibrium to which the stuff of the noosphere tends to drift and fix. But this is impossible for two reasons. First, permanent though they appear in relation to our life-span, the physico-chemical elements, as we now know, are themselves in process of breaking up; there is a death of matter. Moreover, and this is more serious still, formless energy to which the pantheisms of the inanimate try to cling as the basis of stability in no way resembles (even supposing it to be indestructible) the ideal legitimately expected by our conscious endeavours. Born of a dispersion or general release of things, pure matter stands at the antipodes of the 'centre of psychic convergence' required and foreshadowed by all the inner demands and by all the recorded developments of the noosphere. What death, in order to be death no longer, must let through, is not a residue but the most precious essence of our beings; not the most primitive and the most unconscious, but the most evolved and the most reflective parts of ourselves. And each of us, by the long labour of the past in the first place, and secondly, thanks to our individual liberty, is gradually forming a nucleus for vision and action, an 'I', a *person*.

In the interest of the world itself, to be preserved in us, the final establishment of this very element is of prime importance. In us cosmic evolution is a work of *personal* nature. It cannot possibly end, either in itself or in our consciousness of its progress, except in an element of personal form, into which in some way or another our personalities will flow: precisely in the 'common soul' that the totalizing organization of human energy allowed us just now to foresee.

But at this very point a contradiction appears. A centre of personal stuff totalizing in itself the essence of our personalities; this comes to be the definition, as we gradually see it more clearly, of the universal centre of attraction, recognized as necessary if the impetus of the noosphere is to be sustained. Now are these properties mutually incompatible? Can a universal still be personal, and can what is personal be communicated to another person (in order to be totalized in him) without thereby becoming depersonalized, that is to say destroyed? A double difficulty, the solution of which will once and for all illumine the underlying laws of human energy.

1. The idea in common circulation that the universal is opposed to the personal, seems to have its instinctive origin in the fact that 'personality' only manifests itself to our experience in connexion with individuals, and its scientific origin in the modern discovery of those vast diffused unities of energy and matter, in which, as we have said, it has been possible for us to believe we have found the stable and definite form of the All. But this idea (we ought rather to say this impression) does not stand up to analysis. The totality of a sphere is just as present in its centre, which takes the form of a point, as spread over its whole surface; in fact it really lies only in that point. Now why should it be strange for the universe to have a centre, that is to say to collect itself to the same degree in a single consciousness, if its totality is already partially reflected in each of our particular consciousnesses? To conceive of an ultimate centre of thought is after all only a matter of extending along the same line the process by which the human soul was born.[1] In order that, in a given world, the appearance of a personal-universal not only can but must take place, it is sufficient for the world in question to be 'structurally convergent'. That our universe is precisely of such a structure is revealed by the very existence of our individual centres of thought.

2. We are now faced with the second aspect of the paradox. To establish the possibility, and even the necessity, of a personal-universal at the summit of evolution, we have just assumed that an ultra-concentration in a higher consciousness could and must be produced from human personal elements. But is such a transformation in fact intrinsically realizable? At first it would seem that it is not. At a first view, we can only see two imaginable processes which could lead to the formation of a universal centre: either the absorption of the lower centres in a more powerful

[1]In so far as the existence of the soul, in the course of development of creation, is linked with the appearance of the body. (*Ed.*)

unity that will absorb them, or a coalescence of these centres in a resulting unity born of their assemblage. Now neither of these two mechanisms shows itself capable of assuring, as would be necessary, a progress of the elements *in cohesion* and *in distinction at once*. By nature, the elementary 'I's', once formed, can no longer advance in being except by an increase of the interior concentration from which they were born. How therefore could they be absorbed or melt into anything without proportionately shrinking back on themselves? We have accepted that, to be more personal, the human nuclei would have to unite in another or among themselves. But the point is that they cannot fuse without, apparently, to the same extent contracting their personality. Is it possible to escape this contradiction? Yes, we must reply, and indeed very easily. In order to see the paradox vanish, it is sufficient to turn the last, fallacious proposition upside down. One personality, we have just said, seems unable to join itself with another personality except by losing something of its own personality. But precisely the reverse is true. Let us observe any unification by *convergence* that operates in the field of our experience: a grouping of cells in a living body, a grouping of individuals and functions in a social organism, a grouping of souls under the influence of a great love. And we come to a factual conclusion that easily proves the theory. It is this: the phenomena of fusion or dissolution are in nature only the sign of a return to fragmentation in homogeneity. Union, the true upward union in the spirit, ends by establishing the elements it dominates in their own perfection. *Union differentiates*. In virtue of this fundamental principle, elementary personalities can, and can *only* affirm themselves by acceding to a psychic unity or higher soul. But this always on one condition: that the higher centre to which they come to join *without mingling together* has its own autonomous reality. *Since there is no fusion or dissolution of the elementary personalities the centre in which they join must necessarily be distinct from them, that is to say have its own personality.*

Hence we have the following formula for the supreme goal

towards which human energy is tending: an organic plurality the elements of which find the consummation of their own personality in a paroxysm of mutual union and limpidity: the whole body being supported by the unifying influence of a *distinct centre* of super-personality.

This last condition or qualification has considerable importance. It demonstrates that the noosphere in fact *physically* requires, for its maintenance and functioning, the existence in the universe of a true pole of psychic convergence: a centre different from all the other centres which it 'super-centres' by assimilation: a personality distinct from all the personalities it perfects by uniting with them. The world would not function if there did not exist, somewhere ahead in time and space, 'a cosmic point Omega' of total synthesis.

Consideration of this Omega will allow us to define more completely, in a concluding chapter, the hidden nature of what we have till now called, vaguely enough, 'human energy'.

VI LOVE, A HIGHER FORM OF HUMAN ENERGY

We have just recognized that by hominization the universe has attained a higher level on which its physico-moral powers gradually take the form of a fundamental affinity, binding the individuals to one another and to what we have called the 'Omega point'. In us and around us, we have been able to conclude, the world's units are continually and increasingly personalizing, by approaching a goal of unification, itself personal; in such a way that the world's essential energy definitely radiates from this goal and finally flows back towards it; having confusedly set the cosmic mass in motion, it emerges from it to form the noosphere.

What name should we give to an influence of this sort?

Only one is possible: love.

Love is by definition the word we use for attractions of a personal nature. Since once the universe has become a thinking one everything in the last resort moves in and towards personality, it is necessarily love, a kind of love, which forms and will increasingly form, in its pure state, the material of human energy.

Is it possible to verify *a posteriori* this conclusion which is imposed on us *a priori* by the conditions of functioning and maintenance of the thinking activity of the earth's surface?

Yes, I believe so. And in two different ways.

Psychologically, first, by observing that love carried to a certain degree of universality by a perception of the centre Omega is the only power capable of totalizing the possibilities of human action without internal contradictions.

Then *historically*, by observing that such a universal love actually presents itself to our experience as the highest term of a transformation already begun in the mass of the noosphere.

Let us try to demonstrate this.

A Love, the Totalizing Principle of Human Energy

Those who greet with the greatest scepticism any suggestion tending to promote a general co-ordination of thought on earth are precisely the first to recognize and deplore the state of division in which human energies are vegetating: disconnected actions by the individual, disconnected individuals in society. It is evident, they say, that a vast power is neutralized and lost in this unordered movement. But how can you expect dust like this to cohere? Themselves already divided by nature, these human particles continue to repel one another irremediably. You might perhaps force them mechanically together. But to infuse a common soul into them is a physical impossibility.

The strength and weakness of all these objections to the possibility of some eventual unification of the world seem to depend on the fact that they insidiously exaggerate appearances which are only too real, without being willing to take into account certain new factors already perceptible in humanity. The pluralists always reason as if no principle of connexion existed, or tended to exist, in nature outside the vague or superficial relations habitually examined by common sense and sociology. They are at bottom juridicists and fixists who cannot imagine anything around them except what seems to them always to have been there.

But let us see what will happen in our souls the instant there emerges, at the moment fixed by the march of evolution, the perception of an animated universal centre of convergence. Let us imagine (this is no fiction, as we shall soon state) a man who has become conscious of his personal relations with a supreme personality, to whom he is led to add himself by the entire play of cosmic activities. In such a man, and starting with him, a process of unification has inevitably begun, which will be divided into the following stages: totalization of each operation in regard to the individual; totalization of the individual in regard to himself; and finally, totalization of individuals in collective humanity. All this 'impossibility' taking place naturally under the influence of love.

a Totalization by Love of Individual Actions. In the divided state in which the pluralists consider us (that is to say outside the conscious influence of Omega) we most often act only from a tiny portion of ourselves. Whether eating or working, or doing mathematics or a crossword puzzle, man is only partially engaged in his activity, with only one or another of his faculties. His senses, or his limbs, or his reason function, but never his heart itself. Human action but not the action of a whole man, as a scholastic would say. That is why after a life of highest effort, a scientist or thinker may end up impoverished and desiccated—disillusioned; his mind but not his personality has worked on inanimate objects. He has given himself; he has not been able to love.

Let us now observe the same forms of activity in the light of Omega. Omega, in which all things converge, is reciprocally that from which all things radiate. Impossible to place it as a point at the peak of the universe without at the same time diffusing its

147

presence within each smallest advance of evolution. The meaning of this is nothing less than this: that *for him who has seen it* everything, however humble, *provided it places itself in the line of progress*, is warmed, illumined and animated, and consequently becomes an object to which he gives his *whole* adhesion. What was cold, dead, impersonal for him who cannot see, becomes charged for those who see not only with life but with a stronger life than theirs; in such a way that they feel themselves seized and assimilated, as they act, to a far greater degree than they themselves are seizing and assimilating. Where the former only finds an object with limited reactions, the latter are able to expand with the totality of their powers—to love the lowest of their tasks as passionately as if they could touch or caress it. In the external appearance of the operation there is no change. But what a difference in the stuff of the action, in the intensity of the gift! The whole distance between consumption and communion.

And this is the first step in totalization. Within a world of personal and convergent structure, in which attraction becomes love, man discovers that he can give himself boundlessly to everything he does. In the least of his acts he can make an entire contact with the universe, with the whole surface and depth of his being. Everything has become a complete nourishment to him.

b Totalization of the Individual on Himself by Love. That each of our separate pursuits can become *total* under the animating influence of Omega is already a marvellous utilization of human energy. But no sooner has this first transfiguration of our activities taken shape than it tends to enlarge into another more profound metamorphosis. By the very fact that they become total, each one in itself, our activities are logically led to totalize, merged together in a single act. Let us see how.

The immediate effect of universal love, rendered possible by Omega, is to attach to each of our actions a root identity of passionate interest and devotion. What will the influence of this common ground (one might call it this new climate) be on our inner life? Shall we dissolve under its pleasant warmth? Will it blur the clear outline of the objects around us with an atmosphere of mirage? Will it take our attention from the individual and tangible, to absorb us in a confused sense of the universal? If we fear this, it is because we have again forgotten that in the direction of spirit union differentiates. It is undoubtedly true that once I have discovered Omega, all things become for me in some ways the same thing; so that whatever I do I shall have the impression of doing one and the same thing. But this fundamental unity has nothing in common with a melting into homogeneity. In the first place, far from weakening, it accentuates the outline of the elements it assembles; for Omega, the sole object of desire, only forms for our eyes and offers itself to our touch in the completion of those elementary advances by which the fabric of evolution is empirically taking shape. But there is more to it than this. Love not only impregnates the universe like an oil that will revive its colours. It does not simply bind the clouded dust of our experiences into a common lucidity. It is a true *synthesis* which operates on the grouped bundle of our faculties. And this is indeed the point which it is most important to understand.

In the superficial course of our existences, there is a difference between seeing and thinking, between understanding and loving, between giving and receiving, between growing and shrinking, between living and dying. But what will happen to all those contradictions once their diversity has revealed itself in Omega as an infinite variety of forms of a single universal contact? Without any sort of radical disappearance they will tend to combine into a common sum, in which their still recognizable plurality will burst forth in ineffable riches. Not any sort of interference, but a resonance. Why should we be surprised? Do we not know, at a lesser degree of intensity, a similar phenomenon in our own experience? When a man loves a woman with a strong and noble passion that exalts his being above its common level, that man's life, his powers of feeling and creation, his whole universe, are definitely held and at the same time sublimated by his love of that woman. But however necessary the woman may be to that man, to reflect, reveal, transmit and 'personalize' the world for him, she is still not the centre of the world! If therefore the love of one unit for another is powerful enough to melt (without fusing) the multitude of our perceptions and emotions into a single impression, how great must be the vibration drawn from our beings by their encounter with Omega?

Indeed we are called by the music of the universe to reply, each with his own pure and incommunicable harmonic. When, as love for the All advances in our hearts, we feel stretching out beyond the diversity of our efforts and desires the bounding simplicity of an urge in which the innumerable shades of passion and action mingle in exaltation without ever becoming confused, then, within the mass formed by human energy, we shall each approach the plenitude of our powers and personality.

c Totalization by Love of Individuals in Humanity. The transition from the individual to the collective is the present crucial problem confronting human energy. And it must be recognized that the first steps towards its solution only increase our consciousness of its difficulties. On the one side the ever tighter network of economic links, together with an indubitable biological determinism, inevitably presses us against one another. On the other, in the course of this compression, we seem to feel the most precious part of ourselves—our spontaneity and liberty—perishing. Totalitarianism and personalism: contrary to our theoretical expectations, must these two functions necessarily vary in inverse proportion to one another? In order to build the future (for we must certainly go forward) have we to choose between the Charybdis of collectivism and the Scylla of anarchy, between a mechanizing symbiosis and a devitalizing dispersion, between a termite colony and the Brownian movement? This dilemma, long evident to the clear-sighted, seems now suddenly to be entering the field of public notice. For the last year there has been no review or conference in which the question has not been broached. But the outline of a good solution has, alas, never been put forward.

The reason, in my opinion, for the disturbing checks suffered by humanity during the last century in its efforts to organize itself are not to be attributed to some natural obstacle inherent in the undertaking itself, but in the fact that the attempts at grouping are made by inverting the natural order of factors of the projected union. Let me explain.

To totalize without depersonalizing. To save the assemblage and the units at the same time. Everyone agrees that this is the dual task to be accomplished. But how do present-day social groups (democrats, communists, fascists) rate the values they theoretically agree in wishing to preserve? They all consider the individual as secondary and transitory, and place the primacy of the pure totality at the head of their programmes. In all the systems of human organization battling before our eyes, it is assumed that the final state towards which the noosphere is tending is a body without an individualized soul, a faceless organism, a diffuse humanity, an *Impersonality*!

Now once this point of departure is accepted, it vitiates the whole subsequent progress of the operation to the extent of making it impractical. In a synthesizing process, the character finally impressed on the unified elements is necessarily that which permeates the active unifying principle. The crystal assumes geometrical form, the cell animates the matter that joins it. If the universe is tending finally to become *something*, how can it keep a place in itself for *Someone*? If the peak of human evolution is regarded as impersonal by nature, the units accepting it will inevitably, in spite of all efforts to the contrary, see their personality diminishing under its influence. And this is exactly what is happening. The servants of material progress or of racial entities may try their hardest to emerge into freedom, but they are fatally sucked in and assimilated by the determinisms they construct. Their own machinery turns them into machines. The true Hindu karma. And at this moment all that remains to control the machinery of human energy is the use of brute force—the same force that is very logically being offered us at present as an object of worship.

Now this is treason against the spirit, and at the same time a grave mistake in human technology. A system formed of elements of consciousness can only cohere on a basis of immanence. Not force but love above us; and therefore, *at the beginning*, the recognized existence of an Omega that makes possible a universal love.

The mistake, as we have said, of modern social doctrines is to present enthusiasts for human effort with an *impersonal* humanity. What would happen on the day we recognized, instead of this blind divinity, the presence of a conscious centre of total convergence? Then by the opposite determinism to the one against which we are struggling, individualities, caught in the irresistible current of human totalization, would feel themselves strengthened by the very movement that brings them together. The more they grouped themselves under a personality, the more forcibly they would themselves become personal. And quite naturally, without effort, by virtue of the properties of love.

We have already several times stressed the capital truth that 'union differentiates'. Love is only the concrete expression of this metaphysical principle. Let us imagine an earth on which human beings were primarily (and even in a sense exclusively) concerned with achieving global accession to a passionately desired universal being, whom each one would recognize as a living presence in the most incommunicable features of his neighbour. In such a world, constraint would become useless as a means of keeping individuals in the most favourable condition for action, of guiding them in free competition towards better social groupings, of making them accept the restrictions and sacrifices imposed by a certain human selection, of deciding them once and for all not to waste their power of love but to raise it carefully and husband it for the final union. Under these conditions life would finally escape (supreme liberation) from the tyranny of material coercions; and a personality of increasing freedom would grow up without opposition within the totality.

'Love one another.' Those words were pronounced two thousand years ago. But today they sound again in our ears in a very different tone. For centuries charity and fraternity could only be presented as a code of moral perfection, or perhaps as a practical method of diminishing the pains or frictions of earthly life. Now since the existence of the noosphere, on the one hand, and the vital necessity we are under of preserving it, on the other, have been revealed to our minds, the voice which speaks takes on a more imperious tone. It no longer says only: 'Love one another in order to be perfect', but adds, 'Love one another or you perish'. 'Realistic' minds are welcome to smile at dreamers who speak of a humanity cemented and armoured no longer with brutality but with love. They are welcome to deny that a maximum of physical power may coincide with a maximum of gentleness and goodness. Their critical scepticism cannot prevent the theory and experience of spiritual energy from combining to warn us that *we have reached a decisive point in human evolution*, at which the only way forward is in the direction of a common passion, a 'conspiration'.

To go on putting our hopes in a social order obtained by external violence would simply mean to abandon all hope of carrying the spirit of the earth to its limits.

Now human energy, being the expression of a movement as irresistible and infallible as the universe itself, cannot possibly be prevented by any obstacle from freely reaching the natural goal of its evolution.

Therefore, despite all checks and all improbabilities, we are inevitably approaching a new age, in which the world will throw off its chains and at last give itself up to the power of its inner affinities.

Either we must doubt the value of everything around us, or we must utterly believe in the possibility, and I should now add in the inevitable consequences, of universal love.

What are these consequences?

So far, in our study of the socio-totalizing love of human energy, we have principally considered its singular property of joining and articulating the thinking molecules of the noosphere without turning them into machines. But this is only the negative face of the phenomenon. Love has not only the virtue of uniting without depersonalizing, but in uniting it ultra-personalizes. From this pass that we have reached, what horizons appear before us in the skies of humanity?

Here, we must first of all look backwards, to the point where we left the individual human nucleus, at the completion of its transformation by love. Under Omega's influence, we said, each separate soul becomes capable of breathing itself out in a single act into which the incalculable plurality of its perceptions and activities, its sufferings and desires, pass without confusion. Well, the sum of elementary energies constituting the global mass of human energy seems to be moving towards an analogous metamorphosis of a far higher order. We have followed, in the individual, the gradual assumption of the emotions, aspirations and actions in an indefinable operation *sui generis*, which is all these things at once and something more as well. The same phenomenon, on an incomparably greater scale, tends to take place under the same Omega influence in terrestrial thought collected as a whole. And indeed when the whole of humanity, operating and experiencing at the same time with its exploratory surface the centre towards which it is converging; when the same fluid passion suffuses and connects the free diversity of attitudes, points of view and efforts, each represented in the universe by a particular unit of the human myriad; when the overflowing multitude of individual contradictions harmonizes in the profound simplicity of a single desire; what is all this but the genesis of a *collective and unique action*, in which, in the sole conceivable form of love, the powers of personality comprised in the noosphere are realizing themselves, as they approach maturity, that is to say their final confluence?

Totalization of total human energy in a total love.

The ideal glimpsed in their dreams by the world technicians.

This, psychologically, is what love can do if carried to a universal degree.

But is this miracle *really* moving towards realization?

If it is, some traces of this prodigious transformation must be perceptible in history. Can we recognize them? This is what I have still to seek and show.

B Love, the Historical Product of Human Evolution

The above analysis of the synthesizing power of love over the inner life was not made, and indeed could not be made, without some visible model.

Where then in nature today does a first sketch, a first approach to the total act of which we were apparently dreaming exist? Nowhere more clearly, I think, than in the act of Christian love as it can be performed by a modern believer for whom the creation has come to be expressed in terms of evolution. In such a man's eyes, the world's history bears the form of a vast cosmogenesis, in the course of which all the threads of reality converge without fusing in a Christ who is at the same time personal and universal. Strictly and unmetaphorically, the Christian who understands both the essence of his creed and nature's linkages in time and space finds himself in the fortunate position of being by all his various activities and in union with the crowd of his fellows, capable of surrendering to a unique act of communion. Whether he lives or dies, *by* his life and *by* his death, he in some sense completes his God[1], and is at the same time mastered by Him. In short, comparable in every way to the Omega point which our theory led us to foresee, Christ (provided He reveals Himself in the full realism of His incarnation) *tends to produce exactly* the spiritual totalization that we expected.

[1] The mystical body of Christ: 'May they all be one. Father, may they be one in us as you are in me and I am in you' (John 17, 21). (*Ed.*)

In itself the existence, even in detachment, of a state of consciousness endowed with such riches would bring, if fully established, a substantial verification of the views that we have set out on the ultimate nature of human energy. But it is possible to push the demonstration very much further by observing that the appearance in man of the love of God, understood in the fullness that we give it here, is not a simple sporadic accident, but appears as the regular product of a long evolution.

Let us try, before defining the profound significance of the fact, to sketch in broad outline the human history of universal love.

a The Phenomenon of Christianity. Central to the process leading to the recent establishment of an affective relationship of a personal order between man and the universe, we must inevitably place the influence of Christianity (whether we believe or not in its transcendent value).

The phenomenon of Christianity seems to me to have been obscured by the way in which men have often tried to define it by certain characteristics which are only accidental or secondary to it. Simply to present the teaching of Christ as an awakening of man to his personal dignity or as a code of purity, gentleness and resignation, or again as the starting point of our western civilization, is to mask its importance and make its success incomprehensible by ignoring its characteristically new content. The essential message of Christ, I should say, is not to be sought in the Sermon on the Mount, nor even in the drama of the Cross; it lies wholly in the proclamation of a 'divine fatherhood' or, to translate, in the affirmation that God, a personal being, presents Himself to man as the goal of a personal *union*. Many times already (and especially at the dawn of the Christian era) the religious gropings of humanity had drawn near to this idea that God, a spirit, could only be reached by spirit. But it is in Christianity alone that the movement achieves its definitive expression and content. The gift of the heart in place of the prostration of the body; communion beyond sacrifice; God as love, and only to be finally reached in love; this is the psychological revolution, and the secret of the triumph of Christianity. Now since this initial illumination the flame has never ceased to grow.

To estimate the importance of the Gospels' success at its true value is difficult so long as we have not clearly defined the essential nature of the phenomenon of Christianity. In what proportion has the world been 'converted', and to what extent is it being converted still? This is very hard to say. Amidst the numberless vicissitudes and proliferations that mark the Church's development, the historian loses himself and hesitates, much as the natural scientist loses his way among the confused multiplicity of animal forms to the extent of even wondering if there really is a positive movement of life around him. But just as the eye of the natural scientist (if he decides to seek the true constant of evolution in the growth of consciousness) discovers the thrust of a continually mounting stem among the accidental thicket of living species, so the historian of religions, once he decides to measure the march of Christianity not only by the numerical expansion of the faithful but by the *qualitative evolution of an act of love* finds himself tracing the curve of an undoubted progress.

Now let us understand a further point. The growth of the human collective consciousness at present taking place does not prevent there having been in the world before us (in a *not too* distant past) men better endowed as individuals than many of our contemporaries, nor would I affirm that the love of God did not have in Paul, Augustine or Teresa of Avila a certain potential richness that we should have difficulty in finding in any Christian living today. What I mean is that under the influence of rare passions like those of Paul, Augustine or Teresa, the theory and practice of total love have ever since Christ been continually clarified, transmitted and propagated. So, as a result of the two thousand years of mystical experience that support us, the contact we can make with the personal centre of the universe has gained as much in manifest riches as our possible contact with the world's natural spheres after two thousand years of science. Christianity, I would dare to say, is neither more nor less than a 'phylum' of love in nature. Now regarded from this point of view, not only is it not stationary, but it is so much alive that at this very moment we can directly observe it undergoing an extraordinary mutation by raising itself to a steadier consciousness of its universal value.

b Towards a Christian Monism[1]. We have already had occasion to indicate, among the signs that betray a *present* movement of the noosphere, the growth on earth of a certain 'cosmic sense', by which each one of us tends to be habitually and practically conscious of his links with the universe in evolution. In this active participation of our beings in a collective task (a task whose reality is visible at the end of every scientific avenue) the nebula of ancient pantheisms condenses and takes shape at the heart of the modern world. Instinctive, sentimental and passive acceptance of the cosmic powers is succeeded, in men now living, by the rational devotion and reflective collaboration of the unit in a common undertaking and ideal.

Such a rising of the All above the horizon of our individual preoccupations has been interpreted as a sign that Christianity is approaching its natural end. Is not the anthropomorphic form of worship, based on faith in a personal God, about to be replaced by the cult of totalitarian realities like the world and humanity?

The present situation and the probabilities for tomorrow both appear to me very different.

No object, as we have already recognized, could claim to totalize the energy of humanity on itself unless it possessed a soul and was 'someone'. Remaining in the condition of impersonal collectivities, earth and humanity are therefore definitely powerless to support and maintain the spiritual vigour of the world.

[1]In speaking of Christian *monism* or Christian *pantheism*, Teilhard intends to denounce the heretical deviations which remain attached to these words and to bring them back or raise them to their true and orthodox meaning. (*Ed.*)

So long as they remain inchoate the tide raised by their gravitational pull is certainly destined to fall back formlessly on the beach. Both must assume a definite form. But precisely why should they not both succeed in taking soul and personality by drawing near to the God whom they seemed about to abolish? Why should the missing peak of their massive limitlessnesses not prove to be precisely the point already fixed by Christian aspirations?

In fact, by the inevitable play of the psychological forces now active, the synthesis of the two elements is in course of taking place before our eyes. On the one hand the risen Christ of the Gospel can be maintained in the consciousness of the faithful, above a creation that He must by definition consummate, only by incorporating the evolution that some have used as an argument against Him. On the other hand, this same evolution, in order to satisfy the needs of a reflective action born of its transformations, seeks anxiously in the heart of each one of us for a universal centre of thought and affection. Here a sphere calling for a centre. There a centre awaiting a sphere. Far from contradicting one another, as might be feared, the two stars of totality and personality attract one another within the human soul, with all the force of cohesion that tends to close the universe on itself. A conjunction is therefore inevitable. Now from this eventual conjunction the greatest of phenomena will follow: the total sap of things will break in a single heart; man will cherish the world as a person and more than a person; a love will be born for the first time on earth as great and strong as the universe.

This, as we have already said, is the feeling that the most watchful of believers are already beginning to know. But it is also, as we foreshadowed, the fruit of a development taking place in the whole of human thought. If a Christian can today say to his God that he loves Him with his whole body and soul, and with the *whole universe*, he is not making a sudden and individual discovery; his act is the *manifestation* of a new and general *state* of the noosphere. In the growing riches of its formulation, love not only totalizes the psychological resources of the world at a given moment, but illumines and resumes all the efforts of the past; the two expected conditions by which we could recognize that it truly represents the higher form sought by human energy.

Whence emerges, lastly, the following suggestion.

At two critical points human energy has already assumed the form in which we know it today: first the appearance of life, whence emerged the biosphere; then emergence of thought which produced the noosphere.

Cannot a further and final metamorphosis have been in progress since the birth of love in Christianity: the coming to consciousness of an 'Omega' in the heart of the noosphere—the circles' motion towards their common centre: *the appearance of the 'Theosphere'*?

A dream and a fantasy, it will be said. But it fits singularly well with the march of things.

And is it not a strange coincidence moreover that, taken in the cold strictness of its Catholic claims, Christianity (and this explains its struggles to keep jealously free of sects, races, nations and empires) has never claimed to be anything less or anything else but this?

Unpublished, 6 August—8 September, 1937, Marseilles-Shanghai.

APPENDIX: THE PRINCIPLE OF THE CONSERVATION OF PERSONALITY

As an axiom, an epitome and a corollary, all at once, of the above views on human energy, a principle of universal value appears to emerge from our outer and inner experience of the world, which might be called the 'principle of the conservation of personality'.

1. At a *first stage*, the law of conservation of personality only states that the rise of spirit in the universe is an *irreversible* phenomenon.

From each new summit of consciousness that it reaches, the world never again descends. Life having once appeared in matter, the cosmos can never afterwards become 'devitalized', any more than, once life has given birth to thought, it can ever become 'de-hominized'. Taken as a whole, consciousness can advance but not retreat.

'Conservation (without regression) of the highest stage of personalization acquired at each moment by life in the world': under this *qualitative form*, the principle suggested seems to be confirmed by all that we at present know about the historical development of nature.

2. At a *second stage*, the principle of the conservation of personality suggests that a *certain quantum* of energy, in the impersonal state, is engaged in the evolution of the universe, and that it is destined to be transmuted entirely into a personal state at the end of the transformation (the quality of this 'personal end-product' being moreover a function of the quality of 'impersonal' material engaged at the beginning of the process).

'Conservation (without loss), in the course of the spiritualization of the universe, of an undefined amount of power or cosmic "stuff"': under this absolute, *quantitative form* the law of conservation of personality is not directly capable of demonstration, perhaps because it refutes our formal knowledge that we are able to measure the world by 'cubing' it, perhaps because we do not yet see how to express the coefficient of transformation from impersonality to personality. But the principle has nevertheless a use: it states that the spiritualization taking place in the cosmos must be understood as a *change of physical state* in the course of which a certain constant is preserved throughout the metamorphosis.

Understood in this way, let us observe, the conservation of personality in no way implies (quite the contrary) an 'ontological' identity between the unconscious and the self-conscious. Although subjected to a 'quantic' law, personalization remains in effect essentially an evolutionary transformation, that is to say continually the generator of something entirely new. 'So much matter is needed for so much spirit; so much multiplicity for so much unity. Nothing is lost, yet everything is created.' This is all that is affirmed.

3. Finally at a *third stage*, the principle of the conservation of personality signifies that each individual nucleus of personality, once formed, is for ever constituted as 'itself'; so that, in the supreme personality that is the crown of the universe, all elementary personalities that have appeared in the course of evolution must be present again in a distinct (though super-personalized) state.

'Permanence' (immortality) of individual personalities in this numerically third form. The 'conservation of personality' is immediately deduced from forms 1 and 2 (qualitative and quantitative), if one takes account of the fact that each elementary person contains something *unique and untransmittable* in his essence. If this incommunicable quality were to be annihilated by the destruction of a single person, the universe would *ipso facto* cease to integrate the totality of its spiritual powers in its end-product, either in quality or in quantity.

In a universe where spirit is considered *at the same time* as matter, the principle of the conservation of personality appears as the most general and satisfactory expression of the invariance of the cosmos first suspected and sought by physics on the side of the conservation of energy.

20 October, 1937, Peking.

THE MYSTICISM OF SCIENCE

If it were not so difficult for us to master events in which we are ourselves concerned, one of the characteristics that would cause us most wonder in the modern world would be the preponderant importance assumed in human activity by the department, or one might say the function, of research. Only a few generations ago, three figures would undoubtedly have been more than enough to cover the number of eccentrics possessed by the demon of discovery. Today an important fraction of civilized humanity devotes its life to investigating the mysteries and possibilities of the universe, while the other fraction, crowded round the arena, follows the vicissitudes of the struggle with anxious interest. The far distant past, the depths of space, the secrets of matter, the springs of life, all these fields, scarcely glanced at yesterday, are at this moment scrutinized with a persistence and learning and a wealth of instruments, which seem destined before long to deflect and absorb the streams of gold and energy which are still lost in the abyss of armaments and war. Besides the giant guns and huge battle-cruisers, there are now the giant telescopes, ultra-powerful electro-magnets, industrial machines for splitting the atom. Research has ceased to be a childish pastime. It has become the solemn, prime and vital occupation of man, now an adult. If only we know how to look at the world around us, this fact would strike us more than any political disturbances or social unrest.

Several 'determinist' explanations could be given for this extraordinary phenomenon of humanity's becoming single-pointed and proceeding irresistibly to a common act of discovery. Need for well-being which drives us continuously in the direction of increasing comfort and easier work. The struggle for life, which compels the individual and the nation to produce always more economically, to open more and more outlets, to be stronger, to be outstanding if they wish to survive. To preserve the equilibrium, that is to say to keep their distance, everyone in every field of life must always travel faster into strange and new territory. The mystery of matter dogs the heels of the spirit. I willingly recognize the importance of these selfish and immobilist factors in the march of progress. But I observe that they do not completely account for what is happening.

What is in fact admirable and surprising in the present-day human attitude to research is that it shows disinterested passion. The modern scientist of course values and makes use of the eminence conferred on him by his eventual discoveries. But even in his eminence he finally values only what may lead him—him or others—to advance still further. Today in the laboratories, one is always 'risking one's skin' when one lays hands on a new microbe or a new ray. And what is one to say of the men who spend their time (as long as they survive) testing new aeroplanes? And what of those who let themselves be lowered alone into the ocean depths or ascend to the stratosphere? Money and renown may tempt gamblers to take foolish risks when they glitter before their eyes. They do not explain the obscure sacrifice of an individual existence, still less the spontaneous devotion of a generation. For this *auri sacra fames*[1] is no longer enough. To know more in order to be capable of more, in order to be more. The force that is at this moment driving man out on to the high seas is not the simple desire to keep what he already has. Psychologically, its only sufficient reason lies in the consciousness, obscure though it may be, of creating something ahead. Rightly or wrongly, modern man has put his interest and hopes in an unbounded destiny beyond himself. And we have now all embarked to explore and conquer that future. Hope in a limitless future: the two essential characteristics of a religion.

[1]'The hideous hunger for gold'. Virgil, *Aeneid*, III, 56.

There is no doubt about it. This faith is seething in the springs of the great nationalist totalitarian movements. Similarly, though on a far greater scale, we must look also to an energy of a religious nature for an explanation of the present state of the thinking earth. In its present form, that is to say in the unanimous movement carrying it towards new horizons of knowledge, humanity is only supported, and can only be supported, by mysticism.

It is this mysticism of science that I wish to analyse here, in its origins, its developments and its future.

I THE FIRST OUTLINES

In a sense everything profoundly human that exists in man today has always been. But in a sense also, this essential and common ground of spirit has been rehandled, recast, 're-born' in us as a result of the historical crises we have passed through. We recognize ourselves in our childhood; but our childhood would neither have foreseen nor understood our maturity. Such is the law of all growth.

It is so in the social sense, in art and in love. It is the same in our sacred pursuit of science.

As soon as man was man, the tree of science began to grow green in the garden of the earth. But only slowly and much later did it flower. And it is only yesterday that we began to enjoy the divine taste of its fruit.

I am not a historian of the sciences. I do not therefore feel myself specially qualified to write a competent and studied essay on the transformation by which man has moved from amateurishness to respect, and from respect to devotion in this matter of research. I do not think I am far wrong however in reducing the preliminary phases of this development to three: esoterism, aestheticism, curiosity, three stages that humanity had to pass through before waking to the modern mysticism for discovery.

a Esoterism. I will seek an example of scientific esoterism in ancient Egypt. Here we are probably among legends. But this legend is so well authenticated that I can certainly use it to explain myself. If we are to believe certain historians a scientific school was born long ago on the banks of the Nile. Many centuries before our era the priests of Isis had already made deep soundings of the secrets of matter by observation and calculation. Let us ignore those fantasies that have made free play with the hidden meaning of the Sphinx and the astronomical marvels of the Pyramids, and merely hold to the general tradition as a symbol. This brings us the memory of an age in which knowledge of the world, ill distinguished from knowledge of the beyond, was still objectively confused with religion. Religious science, indeed, but in a quite different sense from that in which we should speak of a scientific religion today. In those times a single vague notion of something hidden seems to have covered and confused nature and the gods. There was a precocious rationalism, perhaps, in certain people. But more probably high magic at the same time. To imagine the priest-scientist of Egypt, the 'magus' (if this type truly existed), we could think of him as a primitive Faust, fascinated and terrified by the forces he liberates. To lay a trembling hand on hidden powers, in order to seize them and assume them; but no idea of surrendering to them in adoration. Mysteries, but no mysticism.

b Aestheticism. Esoterism was already buried with its secret discoveries beneath the ruins of its temples. Only its attraction to the occult, ineradicable in man, survived when the scientific viewpoint of the Hellenes appeared to replace it. In their rational genius, and even (as is shown in Aristotle and Archimedes among others) in their sense of observation and experiment, the Greeks opened the way to the modern world. Yet if their methods of research foreshadowed and prepared ours, the spirit which impelled them to make their effort was very far from the spirit that animates us. Was not knowledge for the Greek scientist to take the exact measure of the universe, to fix a definable law, the 'canon' by which the structure of the *kosmos* had been once and for all harmoniously regulated? The *kosmos*: the beautiful and regular, without half-lights; something to be achieved, perhaps in detail, but above all something to be admired, like a giant Praxiteles. This word alone, as has often been observed, contains and reveals a whole philosophy of action and a whole ideal of knowledge: the geometrical clarity of a landscape without distances, frozen by the light. If mysticism is based on imprecise and boundless expectations, the Greeks, as a whole, appear to have been the least mystical of men. Being concerned with enjoyment rather than conquest, they do not seem to have expected or hoped for anything ahead, beyond themselves. Their innumerable myths were *all of a static eternity or of the past.*

And this is perhaps why the Greek flower faded so soon.

c Curiosity. To make a further step, a definite one this time towards the appearance of what might be called the great myth of science, we must now go forward to the Renaissance. Driving at and supplanting alchemy, a prolongation of the old esoterism, sixteenth-century scientific thought seems to have imagined that it was rejoining the aesthetic line of Greek reason. It came near to dreaming, in the physical sciences as in art, of a return to the past. Now the strictly and coolly terrestrial viewpoint of Hellas could not be reborn nor be found unchanged in a consciousness that had been renewed in the interval by the Christian revolution. In fifteen centuries, the human soul had profoundly changed. It had opened itself for ever to a religious disquiet which rendered all food tasteless to it that lacked the salt of a higher reality than any yet conquered and possessed.[1] Simultaneously, thanks above all to the progress of optics, new worlds came into sight. Below and above, towards the infinitely small and the infinitely great, all

[1] Based, it is true, rather on a mystical viewpoint than on empirical fact, one finds an astonishing anticipation of our modern views of progress in the Greek Fathers—Irenaeus, for example.

dimensions expanded prodigiously. Under these two conjoint influences, the Greek *kosmos* burst asunder, spatially and morally at the same time; the circumscribed gave place to the limitless. Exclusive preoccupation with the aesthetic organization of a closed world yielded *ipso facto*, therefore, for the pioneers of the Renaissance, to a concern with exploration of the new regions which suddenly opened up for experiment. Science had once and for all ceased to be speculative; it could now be called discovery. And by this change of direction alone, man had already started on the road which would remove him from his own centre to centre him on the universe. But he had not yet a clear consciousness of this metamorphosis. Surprised and a little troubled by his sight of the new horizons appearing before his eyes, he advanced in the belief that he was simply giving himself up to the pleasure of satisfying his curiosity. And then, by insensible gradations, came one of the greatest intellectual events that history has ever recorded: the revelation of time to the human consciousness.

II THE DISCOVERY OF TIME

We should feel very uncomfortable, not to say 'asphyxiated' if we were obliged to return today to the planetary spheres and cubic skies by which some thinkers right into the seventeenth century believed the world to be enclosed. But we should be far more stifled if we had to accept the narrow boundaries into which our ancestors, right up to the nineteenth century, squeezed the ages of the universe, without discomfort. The perspectives of unbounded time with which we fill our lungs have become so natural that we forget how recently and at what cost they were conquered. And yet nothing is more certain: less than two hundred years ago, the world's leading thinkers did not imagine a past and would not have dared to promise themselves a future of more than six or eight thousand years. An incredibly short time; and what is even more disturbing to our minds, a span of simple repetition during which things were conserved or reintroduced on a single plane, and were always of the same kind.

How did our thought manage to escape from this inorganic and narrow frame? By what process, and under what new influences, has our gaze become accustomed, like that of a new-born child, to separating, and then to placing in a definite perspective, the planes of world time? It would be fascinating to analyse this story. For, thanks to the proximity of events, it would reveal the mechanism of that elusive thing which distances almost always conceal from us: a beginning. The apparently fortuitous meeting of factors which might be called independent, but which nevertheless mysteriously converge to produce a co-ordinated effect: this is what I believe it to be. This is what I believe I see in the movement which, in the short space of three or four generations, has transformed the significance and value of science in men's eyes.

First factor: the development of history. The Middle Ages had shown a curious indifference to the investigation and reconstruction of the past. It was materially preserved, of course, in the confused mass of chronicles. But no effort was made to revive and *see* it. Hence the absence, so disconcerting for us in the art of the period, of all local colour. Now since the Renaissance, and in a most marked way since the seventeenth century, a sense of depth and change has appeared in the study of literature, civilizations and, soon afterwards, of nature. 'Standing on the shoulders of the ancients', said Fontenelle, 'we see further than they did.' And Pascal observed more profoundly: 'The series of men may be considered as a single man, living for ever and continuously learning.' Soon, in his *Époques de la Nature*, Buffon glimpsed the successive transformations of the earth, though still telescoped into too thin a layer of time: its geological disturbances, the variations of climate and succession of fauna. Gradually time became differentiated in the human consciousness and extended backwards, thus symmetrically making room for a future.

Now just at the same time—the second factor—physics and chemistry took shape. Since furthest prehistory, man had found no explanation of the properties and structure of matter; and, so far as energy was concerned, he only knew, or only used, the force of his muscles and the labour of animals. But now suddenly, with Lavoisier, and after Papin, he discovered the mystery and mechanical force of fire. One by one, the secrets contained in inanimate or living bodies opened before his mind and provided means of action. Thus the breach was made by which he could escape from his neolithic conditions. And already he could confusedly glimpse the possibility, no longer of seizing by magic but of rationally harnessing, the inexhaustible powers of nature to exploit the future which history was at that moment revealing to him.

And at that precise instant, from another point of the horizon—the third factor—the great wind of the social awakening of human consciousness arose and gathered strength. Hitherto man had lived chiefly in fragmentary groups, indifferent or hostile to one another. Undiscriminatingly, it was accepted that there could be no essential change in the political and economic conditions which governed, and were thought always to have governed, his existence. But now man began to feel vaguely stirring in him the affinities of a universal brotherhood and the hopes of a new organization of the world. By a study of the past, the mist was dispelled, and the high seas could be seen ahead. Thanks to science, the ship was ready to attempt the adventure. Now the crew offered themselves.

So thanks to the fortunate conjunction of three discoveries—discovery of the gradual succession of living forms, destined soon to culminate in the theories of evolution; discovery of energies, a prelude to the modern conquests of space and the 'ether'; discovery of a sense of humanity, awkwardly expressed in the democratic awakening of the masses—there arose in man, at the dawn of the nineteenth century, the notion of an organic duration open to all the ambitions of the sociologist, the engineer and the scientist.

As a proportionate correlative of the two abysses of the infinitely small and the infinitely great, there opened behind and in front two other abysses, not perceived by Pascal, and from them there rose an anthropogenesis in process of development.

The consciousness of progress had just been born, and with it the religion of science.

III THE RELIGION OF SCIENCE

By light of the discovery of time, that is to say of a global and persistent evolution of the universe, man had at last found the secret of the force which had, from the beginning, driven him to search. Instinctively so far, he had followed his inner urge to explore nature, without proper understanding. He had found various provisional explanations for the implacable need of knowledge which haunted him and gave him a vague sense of growth. Now at last he could define it and justify it rationally. No longer only to know out of curiosity, to know for knowing's sake, but to know out of faith in a universal development which was becoming conscious of itself in the human spirit, to know in order to create, to know in order to be. Henceforth science recognized itself as a means of extending and completing in man a world still incompletely formed. It assumed the shape and grandeur of a sacred duty. It became charged with futurity. In the great body, already coming to birth, of a humanity grouped by the act of discovery, a soul was at last released: a mysticism of discovery.

In this lightning-flash, leaping in the heart of man to reveal to him the grandeur and responsibilities of his earthly activities, there was, we must repeat, a definite element of truth. But in all historical developments a place must always be made for successive approximations. No truth, least of all a fundamental one, can find clear expression except by a series of preliminary trials and gropings. It is as if our mind is no more capable than nature of reaching the centre without first going all round it. We cannot be surprised therefore if, in the first stage of its interpretation, the mysticism of progress took on the oversimplified form, which it has now outgrown, of a sort of worship of science.

It is only right to recognize in the religion of science, as expressed at its beginnings in the philosophical dissertations of the *Grande Encyclopédie*, in the positivist conclusions of Auguste Comte or Marx, or in the Christian or semi-Christian aspirations of Lamennais and Renan, a full and noble courage and great sincerity. In surrendering to dreams of a humanity conscious for the first time of the magnitude of its terrestrial task, the men of last century were obeying a fundamental law of life; and from their enthusiasm our modern world was born. Their vision of a universe in progress was essentially right, and we are still living by it. Only—and this is a serious matter—it was vitiated by an error which was nothing less than a complete reversal of perspective. Instead of making the advance of things depend on a higher pole of the spirit, nineteenth-century science imagined it to be supported and limited by the elementary powers of multiplicity. It projected the centre of the world downwards. Its mysticism strayed off into the worship of matter.

The fascination of matter. To be fair, let us say that the temptation to surrender to it must have been very strong for our predecessors, and it is natural that they succumbed. Let us think ourselves back into their place, that is to say to the first moment when living and animate bodies definitely yielded to the scientific pressure of *analysis*. At that moment, in all realms at once, reality, however simple or spiritual it might have seemed, showed itself capable of spatial and temporal breakdown, or reduction to even simpler elements. This was the age when transformism, newly born, thought that it could trace a continuous chain of forms connecting man across the centuries with monocellular beings. This was the time also when, pushing the palaeontological series one degree lower, chemistry threw a bridge between the organic and the inorganic. This was the age too when, including the totality of molecular, cellular and sidereal constructions in its theories, physical science hoped to reduce the forms and energies contained in the universe to calculable movements of invariable masses.

From these initial successes the illusion was bound to spring, as indeed it did, that man had only to press on with the further rational investigation of measurable antecedents, and he would come on the mainspring of nature. The secret of the universe was hidden in the shadows of the past or the mysteries of the atom. Analysis would bring it out. And once the laws of matter were known, man would perfect himself artificially, by his own powers.

This conception of a world entirely explicable and perfectible by pure reason was of course both simple and intoxicating. It resuscitated the old pride of the Titans in the fable. But no one noticed that it was at the same time lowering the heavens that it set out to scale. By reason of the preponderance and primacy accorded to matter, spirit lost its value, and even its reality; so that progress became implicitly deprived of all definite sense and even of a definite course. By its mechanical determinism, and we must add by its somewhat illogical worship of self-sufficient, or even all-powerful man, the 'religion of science', a product of the eighteenth century, closed the very future into which it thought it was launching itself. It limited the hidden powers of what it had discovered and called 'evolution'. It carried within it seeds which would soon produce a dangerous crisis for man's activities.

IV THE INTELLECTUAL AND MORAL CRISIS OF PROGRESS

Exalting though it appeared to the men of last century to view the new horizons of the universe, and simple though it seemed to them to advance towards them, prospects are decidedly different in the world of today. It has become fashionable among many of our contemporaries to criticize and minimize the value and possibilities of science. We smile easily at the religious enthusiasm that our fathers naïvely showed for progress. Or if we still share it, it is considered proper to disguise the fact in order not to be written down as 'naïve' or uncultured.

What is the cause of this reversal, and how shall we judge it?

The discredit into which faith in progress has so rapidly fallen (in a mere half-century) is partially explained by the habitual illusion which causes all new movements to believe at their birth that the ideal object, whose appearance draws them on, is within hand's reach and can be grasped within the space of a generation. Once they make the attempt, however, the real distance of the goal becomes clear. They are then surprised, and cry that it is a mirage. But in the case of the religion of science this error of distance was complicated by a much more dangerous fault of perspective which, as we have already said, made the first believers turn their backs on the rising sun. The nineteenth century had put its faith in matter. Now in three principal directions—physics, biology and sociology—we observed as we have advanced that matter escapes us.

On the basic ground of physics, first of all, it was the growing powerlessness of analysis to find a definite final form of cosmic substance. The atoms themselves broke up under the impact of radio-active energies. A new stage was thus discovered below the infinitely small, itself opening on to regions where determinism seems to lose all mathematical connotation. Mass and time, those two pillars of positivist science, lost their absolute value at a single blow. The stuff of the universe, examined as a close texture, resolved itself into a mist in which reason could no longer possibly grasp, in what remained of phenomena, anything but the forms that it had itself imposed on them. In the final issue, mind found itself once again face to face with its own reflexion. The 'great fixed lower point' vanished from the grasp of materialism.

In the still more critical realm of biology, it was the failure of mechanism to account for the developments of life. Whatever may have been said, it was unimportant in itself that the animal series revealed themselves to paleontology as more complicated and more deep rooted than had at first been thought. The serious thing was that neither in their overall distribution nor in the pattern of their fibres, nor in the structure of their constituents, did they prove explicable by a simple competition of forms, nor by a simple operation of physico-chemical balances. The evidence had to be accepted. On the whole front of the biological disciplines, after a century of attack, living matter had been methodically broken down into its historical, chemical and energetic elements. But it would not allow itself to be reduced to those components *alone*. There, as in physics, science found an impasse or, to be more exact, encountered a void in the direction of matter.

And the disillusion was still more painful in the field of social organization. Science, it had been hoped and proclaimed, would make man moral by making him happy. Was it not enough to know the secret of the body to cure it and make it happy? Once men could produce the goods of the earth economically and distribute them equally, would this not be the coming of what religion once called the kingdom of God? And we know what happened. On the morrow of 1848, Renan, disconcerted by the first miscarriage of humanitarian theory, publicly acknowledged that 'the destiny of man had become darker than ever.' What can we say today? In physics and biology a defeat is muffled by the laboratory walls. But when a check leads to the spilling of blood, doubt and disquiet affect the mass of humanity. In imagining a perfectible universe of hard-working individuals, have we made a mistake?

Indisputably progress has now fallen (around us and perhaps in our hearts) into an intellectual and moral crisis. We are no longer at all certain whether it is possible or good to attempt further advances towards the building of a future for humanity. Some may be bold enough to rejoice at this crisis. Others may be inclined to fall back into the defeatist attitude of the disillusioned Renan: 'Let us continue to enjoy the supreme gift, that we exist and contemplate reality. Science will always remain the fulfilment of the highest desire of our being, curiosity.' And yet, I will again stress the observation that I made at the beginning: the vast effort of investigation and discovery launched on earth a century ago, far from weakening, continues to proliferate and accelerate beneath our eyes. Disturbed by the failure of our first attempts to light and improve the world, some may already be talking of stopping or limiting the attack. In face of this cowardice human consciousness as a whole falls back on its instinctive certainty, almost its infallible belief, in an attitude that commits it ever more deeply to the pursuit of science. Deep within it despite all the doubts that reason may suggest, man's faith in the future is more alive than on the first day. Retreat, he asks? And the universal practice of research answers for him: Never!

What does all this mean?

In my opinion, the conflict in our souls, in which the compulsions of criticism appear to oppose the strong certainties of our drive to action, does not point to a vital error. There can be no question of doubting the essential intuition that in the nineteenth century made us see man as a participant in and servant of some great work at present taking place. By a certain general success, and by the life it has given us, the value of this prospect, thank God, has been steadily confirmed since its birth. On the other hand, and here lies the source of our present troubles, it must be acknowledged that we have not so far succeeded in understanding the faith which inspires us, or in explaining it satisfactorily. As we said at the beginning, some religion is absolutely necessary to explain, justify and extend the psychological state of the world in which we live. Now, following the collapse of a first idol, this religion has just lost the God that it believed it had found. Standing on the ruins of materialism, we find ourselves supported at the present moment only by all the accumulated vigour of our needs and hopes.

Shall we therefore let the holy spirit that moves us stifle?

No. The spirit is there indubitably, since without it the universe, robbed of the courage that gave it life, would become absurd and incomprehensible. All that is needed is to discover its true name.

The religion of science is dead. To take over from it, there *must be a new mysticism*.

Where is it to be found?

V RELIGION IN SCIENCE

In order to understand what I have still left to say, we must turn back for a moment. I have spoken of the discovery of time, and the moral metamorphosis it produced in the realm of scientific values: research ceasing to be a secular occupation, to become a vital and almost sacred function. Now before we go any further, we must observe the reverberations of this intellectual event in the depths of the Christian soul.

No man may serve two masters.

Faced with a sort of spiritual revolution, the first result of which was to make man bow down before himself, it is easy to imagine that Christianity first thought of the Temptation in the Wilderness, and that it initially recoiled in an attitude of disquiet and defence. Accidentally, owing to its materialistic interpretation of the evolutionary movement it had just discovered in the universe, the religion of science took up a hostile attitude to the God of the Gospels. To this challenge believers in the Gospels had necessarily to reply by condemnation. In this way the only too familiar unhappy war between science and religion was born and continued throughout the nineteenth century. Some have chosen to see this war as a conflict between reason and faith, but it was rather a struggle between two rival mysticisms for the mastery of the human heart.

Now it will be seen on reflexion that this state of war required to be resolved in a higher synthesis. Psychologically it produced a situation of constraint, and so could not last. For this reason.

Since its first struggles with paganism the tendency of Christianity's enemies has always been to regard it as an enemy or at least a despiser of humanity. This is a false truth. By his faith, of course, the disciple of Christ is led to place the goal of his hopes higher and farther off than other men. But the vision of this higher goal does not tend to destroy but on the contrary is destined to recast and elevate the aspirations and progress of what Tertullian has called the 'naturally Christian soul'. The Christian —and here is one of the most certain and precious portions of his creed—does not become so by simply negating but by transcending the world to which he belongs. By definition, his religion, if true, can have no other effect than to perfect the humanity in him.

In that case, if there was, as we have agreed, a deeply humanizing intuition in the idea which unfolded in the eighteenth century that each one of us is a conscious and responsible unit in a universe in progress, it was inevitable that this intuition should sooner or later raise an amplified echo in the heart of Christian consciousness. At the first stage, Christianity may well have seemed to exclude the humanitarian aspirations of the modern world. At the second stage, its duty was to correct, assimilate and preserve them. Is this not the stage to which it is coming at present?

The degree to which Christianity teaches and offers a prospect of universal transformation can never be sufficiently stressed. By the Incarnation God descended into nature to 'super-animate' it and lead it back to Him: this is the substance of the Christian dogma. In itself, this dogma can be reconciled with many representations of the empirical world. So long, for example, as the human mind saw the universe only as a fixed arrangement of ready-made elements, the Christian had no serious difficulty in introducing the mysterious process of his sanctification into this static assemblage. But was not this, to some extent, a second best? Was a fundamental immobility of the cosmos the best imaginable framework for the spiritual metamorphosis represented by the coming of the kingdom of God? Now that the dust of early battles is dying down, we are apparently beginning to perceive that a universe of evolutionary structure—provided that the direction of its movement is truly located—might well be, after all, the most favourable setting in which to develop a noble and homogeneous representation of the Incarnation. Christianity would have been stifled by a materialist doctrine of evolution. But does it not find its most appropriate climate in the broad and mounting prospect of a universe drawn towards the spirit? What could serve as a better background and base for the descending illuminations of a Christogenesis than an ascending anthropogenesis?

I will not venture any further in this field of theology. But I can vouch for one thing: that for a Christian working in the field of research, scientific activities take on marvellous significance once he reverses the mechanistic point of view and places the principle of movement, which the nineteenth century believed it had discovered at the antipodes to God, in an upper pole of creative attraction. Pascal and his contemporaries could still regard research in physics as an inferior kind of occupation, for which the believer had almost to apologize, a sort of theft from prayer and worship. For the evolutionist who is now a Christian, the barrier which appeared to separate the sacred from the profane can now be overcome. In a universe in which everything makes for the gradual formation of the spirit which God raises to final union, every undertaking acquires, in its tangible reality, the sacred value of a communion. A work which consists in developing our consciousness of the world by means of knowledge partakes in a very real sense of the priestly functions, since it prepares an object for them: their task being to push on still further beneath the creative impulse a universe at whose heart God comes to take His place.

This viewpoint seems to offer contemporary science a complete solution of the intellectual and moral problem with which we are at present wrestling. Not only does a spiritual 'evolutionism' in fact escape the theoretical difficulties encountered by mechanists in the final explanation of matter and life. But in becoming Christian, it also brings to the efforts of human research itself, as it develops and calls for life before our eyes, the full plenitude of the soul it awaited and the mysticism it sought. On the one side those who accept it find their proud assurance preserved and justified, in its entirety: their belief, born of human consciousness, that even the palpable world has a future, and this future is partly in our hands. On the other, since the perfection of the universe coincides with the coming of individual souls to a higher and distinct centre of personality, the evils resulting which have produced the moral crisis of progress are swept aside: boundlessly encouraged in his exploratory efforts, man, if he will be faithful to the end to his urge for discovery, at the same time undergoes a complete readjustment of his inner life. No more fear of mechanization. The reign of brute force is over. No more amorality. Fundamentally no mysticism can live without love. The religion of science believed that it had found a faith, a hope. It has died by excluding Christian love.

I will resume and conclude.

In order to sustain and extend the huge, invincible and legitimate effort of research in which the vital weight of human activity is at present engaged, a faith, a mysticism is necessary. Whether it is a question of preserving the sacred hunger that impels man's efforts, or of giving him the altruism he needs for his increasingly indispensable collaboration with his fellows, religion is the soul biologically necessary for the future of science. Humanity is no longer imaginable without science. But no more is science possible without some religion to animate it. Christianity is an exemplary form of the religion of science. Must I add that it is the necessary form, since earth seems unable to follow the true progress of its activities to the end except by becoming converted? To judge by the repugnance and despair in the face of effort to which especially clear-sighted unbelievers confess today, one might be led to believe so. I would not venture a positive judgement. It remains (and this is the least one can say) that the Christian scientist seems to everyone the best situated and the best prepared to develop in himself and foster around him the new human type seemingly awaited at present for the further advancement of the earth: the seeker who devotes himself, ultimately through love, to the labours of discovery. No longer a worshipper of the world but of something greater than the world, through and beyond the world in progress. Not the proud and cold Titan, but Jacob passionately wrestling with God.

Études, 20 March, 1939.

INDEX